Let Us
Make A Man

*The Black Man's Guide to Creating
a Life of Significance, Impact & Power*

SPONSORED MOTIVATION

Middletown, DE

Let Us Make A Man: *The Black Man's Guide to Creating a Life of Significance, Impact & Power*

ISBN 978-1-952870-05-7 (paperback)
ISBN 978-1-952870-06-4 (epub)
Library of Congress Control Number: 2021903839

For permission, information requests, and bulk orders, write to the publisher at hello@spoonfedmotivation.com Subject: Spoonfed Motivation Publications.

Scripture quotations taken from the Amplified® Bible (AMP), Copyright © 2015 by The Lockman Foundation. Used by permission. www.lockman.org.

Scripture quotations marked ESV are taken from The Holy Bible, English Standard Version® (ESV®), Copyright © 2001 by Crossway, a publishing ministry of Good News Publishers. All rights reserved. ESV Text Edition: 2016

Scriptures marked KJV are taken from the KING JAMES VERSION (KJV): KING JAMES VERSION, public domain.

Scripture quotations marked NIV are taken from THE HOLY BIBLE, NEW INTERNATIONAL VERSION®, NIV® Copyright © 1973, 1978, 1984, 2011 by Biblica, Inc.® Used by permission. All rights reserved worldwide.

Scripture quotations marked NKJV are taken from the New King James Version®. Copyright © 1982 by Thomas Nelson. Used by permission. All rights reserved.

Scripture quotations marked NLT are taken from the *Holy Bible*, New Living Translation, copyright © 1996, 2004, 2015 by Tyndale House Foundation. Used by permission of Tyndale House Publishers, Inc., Carol Stream, Illinois 60188. All rights reserved.

Legal Disclaimer: This book is for informational purposes only. The authors make no claims or guarantees. The content in this book should not be considered as counseling, medical, legal or other professional advice. The intent of the authors is to offer information of a general nature to help you in your quest for emotional, physical, and spiritual development and well-being. In the event you choose to act on the information in this book, you do so at your own discretion, and the authors and publisher assume no responsibility for your actions.

Visionary: Dr. Cherita Weatherspoon
Compiled by: Anwar L. Miller and Corban I. Weatherspoon with Dr. Cherita Weatherspoon
Cover Design: Muda Grafika
Interior Design: Amit Dey

Dedication

To Solomon, Ian and Jaden, our sons and brothers, you are kings. Take dominion over the land our God has given you. Seek to be righteous over right. Be productive and prosperous so you can leave a legacy of impact and an inheritance to your sons and daughters. Be a unifier and contribute to the larger community. This is your mission as well as your birthright.

Table of Contents

Introduction

Our Black men are dying and no one seems to care. Our Black men are crying and no one sees their tears. Our Black men are trying and no one honors their efforts. Our Black men are succeeding and no one wants to share.

···✦✦···

*L*et Us Make A Man: The Black Man's Guide to Creating a Life of Significance, Impact & Power was written for Black men of all ages, across the African diaspora, to help us navigate life in this world as Black men. A life that has been historically devalued, demoralized, degraded, demonized, detested, disdained, deplored, deprived, and dehumanized.

That may be the story but it is not who we are.

Black men—our fathers, our brothers, our sons, our friends—are powerful kings who were stripped from our kingdoms but are positioned to step onto the throne and reclaim what is rightfully ours. The writings in this book will help prepare our brothers for the elevation that is long overdue. Birthed through personal experiences, the words of our authors provide guidance, wisdom, hope, and acknowledgment.

The formation of this book was guided by Genesis 1:26-28 (NKJV) and the core principles of these verses: exercise dominion, reflect righteousness, be prosperous, and unite community. The book is divided into four sections based on these principles, and each section includes chapters that will educate, enlighten, and empower readers in these areas. Each chapter shares a lesson on a specific character trait, commitment, goal, or behavior that we believe is essential for Black men to embody so we can lead in our homes, in the community, and in the workplace; build and leave a legacy of impact and influence, and be productive contributors to our families and society.

Brothers, it's time to take our rightful positions as kings and to help prepare future generations to stand in our place when it's their time.

EXERCISE DOMINION

"Rulership is in our genes, dominion is in our makeup. We were designed to rule the earth."

Myles Munroe

Mission

You are a perfect mix of strength, ambition, creativity, resilience, love, purpose, and potential. You were created with intention. Created with purpose, for a purpose.

Everyone has their own unique purpose, along with a perfectly crafted path they can venture on to carry out their mission and reach their goals.

At times, we may get discouraged by the enormity of our goals. We may even question if we are equipped enough to fulfill our mission.

Am I good enough?

Can I really accomplish this?

What if I fail?

It's okay to have these thoughts. Standing at the bottom of a mountain with the goal to reach the top will surely render a host of emotions. But realize that, like a seed, you already have everything within you to succeed.

Every step forward builds your endurance to keep progressing. Every challenge provides a lesson that molds you into the best version of yourself. Every win you desire to have is already waiting for you, and the space between where you are now and where you want to be is a kingdom waiting for you to grow into the King that you are.

As Black men, we sometimes feel a resistance weighing us down as we attempt to move forward. We sometimes feel the loneliness in rooms filled with peers that don't look like us. We sometimes are directed to hide parts of us to fit a mold.

The truth is, we find ourselves walking out into a society not created with us in mind. But in that truth, we also find the power we have to change the narrative and create a future that inspires generations to come.

In every sense of the word, we are Creators. Our thoughts and our perspectives matter. Our essence drips of trends that others cannot create naturally. The way we talk, the way we walk, the way we think are worthy enough to be bottled up and imitated across the world. We are that powerful, and we are that important.

As we walk our path towards achieving our goals, it's important to remember the power we have. Whatever we choose to do shapes the future. Although everyone has their unique path to walk and mission to carry out, we are all still connected. By working towards our goals, we provide inspiration to other brothers and sisters doing the same. As we walk our path, we leave behind worlds of possibilities for those coming behind us.

As you discover your purpose, uncover your talents and walk your path to carry out your mission, I leave you with a poem.

Finding your path is beautiful
Whether you stumble upon it
Or you seek it out
Either way, it's always waiting for you

Finding your path is challenging
There are no footsteps to follow
The path is hardly visible
But the more you walk, the more it reveals itself

Walking your path is liberating
It forces you to explore yourself
You are your only obstacle
Only you can block yourself from walking forward
You are your greatest teacher
Your experiences are seeds to learn from

Walking your path takes faith to trust what you can't see
It takes courage to bet on yourself
It takes discipline to stay the course
Even when you stumble off the path
Only you can find your way back

You may feel lonely at times
But you are not alone
Your reason for walking reveals itself
Just as your greatness reveals itself

Abdullah Jose

Vision

"Do not withhold good from those to whom it is due."

Proverbs 3:27 (NKJV)

The experience of receiving a Vision is as close as a man can come to engaging in intimate communication with the All-That-Is. However, it can feel like one of the more annoying and borderline rude instances that a man can ever experience.

The best way to describe it is like being struck by lightning from inside your own mind with no tangible evidence of the event ever having transpired.

No singed clothing, no burn marks, no medical records, and no doctor's note.

To make matters worse, instead of being neurologically traumatized (a good reason to call out sick or to have someone call out sick on your behalf), what happens next is very much the opposite: you now have a sentient co-occupant in your mind that requires your full participation and contribution of resources to help them "move out and get their own place." It keeps its own hours, plays its music way too loud, and always interrupts you when you're trying to focus on something else.

What was once any given day that could be filled with not-much-of-anything is now potentially 86,400 seconds of "Ooh, that speaks to who I am! If you get that for me, then it'll help me get my own place that much faster!"

If any of this resonates with you, then congratulations, sir... you are a Visionary.

···◆◆◆···

A vision could be described as a psycho-spiritual convergence of seemingly disparate ideas that gives birth to itself in the mind of a given individual (a Visionary). Similar to the common experience of "having an idea," a vision can present itself to the Visionary with little to no conscious effort. What distinguishes a vision from an idea is the volumes of discernable information that is "gifted" to a given Visionary.

To put it into common technical terms, an idea is equivalent to a highway billboard, whereas a vision is equivalent to gigabytes (sometimes even terabytes) of information planted in one's mind... from within one's mind. The more proficient a person becomes in receiving a vision, the more the interaction takes the form of a symbiotic relationship of sorts.

The strength and integrity of the Visionary's relationship WITH the vision simultaneously IS the Visionary's purpose, gives the Visionary purpose, and casts (or even executes) the vision.

From a certain point of view, a vision can be viewed as the convergence of a multitude of living elements in varying degrees; below are nine examples of those elements:

Clarity	Curiosity	Decisiveness
Empathy	Foresight	Innovation
Intuition	Simplicity	Understanding

With all things that require definitions, it's a time-tested best practice to briefly cover those things that a vision is NOT:

- A vision is NOT a device to be exploited for the purpose of trivial social advantages
  - Example: "Bickering and Bargaining"
- A vision is NOT a construct to be used for the purpose of deflection or evasion
  - Example: "Offloading and Outsourcing"
  - Example: The story of "Jonah and the Whale"
- A vision is NOT a tool to be weaponized for the purpose of socio-cultural encroachment
  - Example: "Liberties and Luxuries"

Your vision is as real as you are. It respects you, trusts you, values your safety, and always seeks to keep the fields of constructive communication open. For all intents and purposes, your vision is your complement… NOT your undoing.

At the same time, your vision will also ensure that you stay true to your designation as Visionary… even when you don't necessarily feel like it.

····◆◆◆···

The textbook definition of visionary is "a person of keen insight;"[1] which, in truth, is correct. However, as with most things, the seemingly obvious answer is obviously deceptive.

In this particular space, the word Visionary (capital V) would be defined as a "Man of Vision;" with special attention paid to the word "of."

1. Used to indicate possession, origin, and association[2]
2. Constituted by, containing, or characterized by[2]

As a Visionary, you are a man who is possessed by and imbued with the same sentient source code (for brevity's sake, let's call it "Force") from which you were spawned.

So, the good news for you is that you're not alone.

There is an indefinite number of Visionaries both throughout history and in our lifetime, some more famous than others, who serve as cultural and spiritual pillars of reference for other Men of Vision. Below are a few:

- Noah
- Francois Toussaint Louverture
- Denmark Vesey

- Reginald Lewis
- Wole Soyinka
- Nelson Mandela
- Guion Bluford

As a Man of Vision, YOU have been gifted a sacred duty and now serve as a critical link in a universal chain.

···•♦•···

Though there may be some comfort in knowing the proper names of others who were tasked (and accomplished) such great work, there is an inevitable sense of disorientation and possible anxiety that comes with the Visionary's first realization...

"All of this is in my head and I'm the only one who can do the work to bring it forward."

For most people who engage in acts of creativity (whether professionally or personally), it's simply a matter of picking up a book (they already own) or going to a store (to which they've already been) and acquiring the resources, processes, and techniques needed to begin transforming their empty page or palette into a reflection of the inspiration that lies just behind their eyes.

Yeah... that's not you; you're a Visionary.

It's almost as if your vision is sitting in a comfortable chair at the opposite end of the living room of your mind, impatiently but quietly waiting for you to pull everything together and make something happen. All of which is happening while you attempt to find some semblance of peace while suppressing the elephant in the room… "Why Me?"

After successfully navigating the quagmire of "why" and arriving at the seemingly impenetrable wall of "how," the mind of the new Visionary inevitably shifts to the space of "when?"

- When do I start?
- When do I make the time?
- When is it "due?"

To address the topic of "when," a good point of comedic reference is a scene from the 1987 movie "Spaceballs."[4] In this example below, you, as Visionary, are essentially Dark Helmet. Colonel Sandurz? He is your vision.

Dark Helmet: What's happening? When does this happen in the movie?

Colonel Sandurz: Now, sir. What's happening now is happening now.

Dark Helmet: What happened to then?

Colonel Sandurz: We passed it.

Dark Helmet: When?

Colonel Sandurz: Just now.

Vision work is all about the now, regardless of your degree of certainty regarding where "here" is. Being present in the now, with respect to your vision (literally) allows the Visionary to see the domain of vision work for what it truly is: an open-world environment of self-actualization under your command.

···◆◆◆···

The events of your life, in conjunction with your decisions at critical points (some people refer to them as "crossroads"), have led you to the stage of Visionary. The tie that binds all Visionaries is that, despite their individual ethnicity, creed, or religious influences, the cumulative experiences and memories in and/or of the world that human males face are encrusted with every gem that is required to impeccably cast a vision. At the moment the vision presents itself, the Visionary is provided with virtual evidence of values: proficiency, diplomacy, precedence, and multidimensionality.

Through repetitive interactions with the vision, one learns to engage the vision work at the 10,000-foot view as well as at a seemingly atomic level. To the Man of Vision terms like "time," "silence," "consciousness" and "unity" are more than mere words; they are a few of many complex extra-sensory systems of a greater System that acts as both a roadmap and skill set for the Man of Vision.

So… how do you cast your vision?

Well, my vision told me to tell you that, as Men of Vision, YOUR "how" is none of MY business.

Now… go cast YOUR vision.

K. Darren Diggs

Authority

Authority is the ability or power to give instruction, to also make decisions in situations, and to enforce a system of order. As men, many of us, if not all of us, have the desire to lead. This may be to lead ourselves, a family, or maybe even a business. In my few years of taking on leadership roles and responsibilities, one of the interesting things that I have discovered while working with people in leadership is that so many want to take on authority, but fail to realize that in order to obtain authority you must first submit to authority. I think this can be difficult for men because it is in our nature to dominate and take control. But, let me help you understand why submitting to authority is important. When you follow directions, people are more willing to trust you. For example, if your CEO instructs you to make an inquiry via email to the CEO of another company and you do so, he or she will know that you are reliable and can get the job done. If you continue to follow through and prove to be diligent and dependable, they may see you fit for a higher ranking position in the company. Or, if your college professor gives you weekly homework assignments to complete, and you turn them in on time, that instructor may offer you an internship because they see that you are responsible.

However, let's say that when your CEO instructed you to send an email to the other CEO, you decided that it would be better to call the CEO to get a quicker response. You call the CEO of the other company and actually get them on the line but you are unable to answer their questions and the call ends with the CEO not wanting to do business with your company. Not only did you fail to follow the instructions given to you (to submit to authority) but you also lost a potential customer. Now, you have to explain to your CEO the mistake that you made. At a minimum, your CEO will question your competency and reliability; at worst, you will face termination. As the student who never hands in your homework assignments on time and is always making excuses as to why you don't have it, you are showing your professor that you have a poor work ethic. How might this play out when you apply for that internship position? In order for people to want to give you authority, you have to demonstrate that you are capable of handling authority, which includes being able to submit to authority.

···✦✦✦✦···

When you do get in a position of authority, you have to know how to honor your position of authority. When I say honor your position of authority, what I mean is that you have to respect yourself by knowing your limits, develop boundaries, not lose yourself in the process, and respect the position that you are serving in. Sometimes, when we are granted the opportunity to lead, we get so caught up in the calling that we forget who we are and why we have been called to that purpose. But no matter the notoriety you receive for your good deeds or accomplishments or how many times people call on you for your wisdom or advice, there should be a level of humility at the core of your being; and in this place of humility, you should be mindful of your limits and what you can handle. And, throughout all of this, remember that your purpose is not for you. It is for everyone that you are connected to; what you are doing is so much bigger than you.

···✦✦✦···

It is easy to lose your way when in a position of authority or power. I think the best way to avoid this is by being self-aware and self-reflective. When we are self-aware, we have an understanding of ourselves and how other people perceive us. Being self-reflective gives us the opportunity to become more self-aware. From personal experience, I think one of the best ways to understand ourselves better is to journal our thoughts. As Black male leaders, we experience many different things in our day-to-day lives, and sometimes it is hard for our brains to process it all. But a cathartic way to understand ourselves better and how we are engaging in the world (or how the world is engaging with us) is to write things down. After journaling your thoughts, you can look back and find clarity around why you do what you do and even begin to identify patterns of thoughts and behaviors that may be working for or against you, thus allowing you to have a greater sense of self. Writing is an important habit to develop when you are in a leadership position. Because so much attention is on you and you are being judged constantly, you have to have a safe space to process that. It's helpful to have a person to do that with, but in the absence of a person, writing can be an effective tool. It is important that we evaluate who we are and how we are showing up in our positions of authority; however, there is more to it. I also believe it is important for us to have accountability partners in our lives. We all have blind spots in our personalities. What I mean is that we have actions and tendencies that we are not conscious of and cannot see—no matter how self-reflective or self-aware we are. I often think of it like this: there are only parts of our face that we can see unless we look into a mirror. The parts of our face that we cannot see are our blind spots; our accountability partners are the mirrors that help us to see what we can't. We need people in our lives who will help us to see certain qualities in ourselves who are not afraid to correct us when we are wrong because they can see the greatness inside of us and do not want us to fail.

···◆◆◆◆···

When you are in a position of authority, you may find that it is difficult for some people to be receptive to your authority. When you are a person that is gifted to lead and orchestrate change in environments, people do not always understand your point of view and why you make the decisions you make. This may cause people to actively work against your ideas. The best way for people to grasp where you are coming from is to properly communicate with those you are leading. As leaders, we have to be willing to keep open and consistent communication with those we are leading so our intent is always clear and we can reassure them of their importance in the process. This may require group bonding exercises or spending one-on-one time with the people who are a part of your team. When you take the time to get to know the people you are leading personally and understand their challenges, they will be more receptive to following the order and structure that you have created for them. If you are a person that is always telling everyone what to do without hearing their ideas or how what you are proposing impacts them, they may be less likely to follow your plan. Taking authority is not always easy, but know that as Black men, we have everything we need to accomplish with authority the responsibilities we've been granted as leaders.

Marco Robinson

Servant Leadership

"How dare he beat me! What kind of dad, won't let his son win?" the young boy roared. He had that look, eyes full of unspent tears, shoulders slumped, defeated. In a precious moment of four generations, great-grandfather winks at Pop-pop and gives that knowing smile. Pop-pop knows what he must do. In a seemingly innocent unfolding of events, I, the man who once watched my own son roil in anger and frustration, am now reliving a familiar scene. This time I am not the father who dealt a blow of defeat, but the Pop-pop with timeless truth that soothes and simmers the seething energy of his grandson.

I have been a part of many things in my life and have worn many hats. Marine, deacon, teammate, manager, mason. I have led and I have followed. Even with all of that, the most important is being part of a family; for that is where greatness is truly formed–to be close to the people and things that anchor you and to have family and close friends with whom we can laugh and remind us of who we are and where we come from. It is in the domain of family that greatness is most remarkably demonstrated by how we learn to serve, support and uplift each other. As men, it is through this expression of servant leadership that our greatest significance is forged and refined and where we can affirm another as truly worthy and highly esteemed, regardless of circumstances.

When I was five, my dad taught me to play chess. He bought me a board and a book for beginners and invited me to play. He then beat me regularly for what felt like forever. He always explained what happened, whether I chose my move badly or if he used a different technique. He always won. It made me angry, "How dare he beat me! What kind of dad, won't let his son win?" I roared. I spent years reading books on chess, practicing chess scenarios and destroying any kid willing to sit across the board from me. I still couldn't beat my dad, though. I was so angry, I complained to my grandfather. "That'll fix him," I thought.

Without even knowing a lesson was being delivered from my grandfather, during those fiery moments I learned patience, control and to trust the wisdom of my elder. I learned to ask questions, then listen for the answers. And, if I didn't understand the answers, to ask more questions and then to listen some more. If I was uncomfortable asking questions, I learned to say I was uncomfortable asking questions and then ask anyway. Then listen some more. He taught me that I could live through defeat and disappointment. Those things didn't define me; I could choose the content of my character and how I would respond to adverse situations. I learned that I was worthy of all the good things God promised.

There came a day that I sat with my own son, Nintendo controllers in hand. The past became present. He was fierce, determined and at times, explosively angry. He still couldn't beat me, though. "How dare he beat me! What kind of dad, won't let his son win?" he roared. Just as my grandfather had done for me, I remember my dad tempering my son's anger and encouraging him to keep fighting to become better. Like a co-conspirator, Pop-pop prodded the young buck to keep working the plan until he could one day claim victory as his own.

By now, I have learned to be a gracious winner, and to accept my defeats with dignity and class. Dad and I occasionally break out an old dusty board. It doesn't really matter who wins; it's the sitting that counts. I have been the boy–the beauty of youth, raw and full of energy–yearning for direction, but unready for the challenges that he will face. Not ready to lead, but not willing to follow easily. I have been the young man, gaining experience and developing into the leader, vigilant and unyielding–the rock upon which so many depended; leading from strength and authority and carrying the weight of the world refusing to be "too soft" on my son, a boy growing up in a world that is often unjust and unforgiving. Today, I am wisdom that guides and directs toward sound reasoning, though never steering the wheel of another man's choice; anticipating trials and challenges, yet standing fast through success and failure to bring out the greatness in another.

As men, the call of true greatness is forged through servant leadership that is most remarkably expressed in the domain of family, oftentimes as a father, but also as an uncle, a grandfather, or even as brother or son. We serve and support the ones we love most, making huge sacrifices in our lives to make their lives better. Though our family connections may not be those shared by birth origins, we come from a shared history and are linked through cultural experiences that have very much influenced who we are. Whether we are called father or friend, we are all our brother's keeper, anchoring each other in the truth of our inherent worth, due respect, and capacity towards unmatched contribution and accomplishment. We must uplift each other through the frustrations of defeat and come alongside one another to help resist resignation and fuel the fire towards mastery and distinction. Each of us must model living lessons for another, but also maintain a willingness to honor and learn from our brothers who have cultivated those skills and attributes we need to refine and develop. This servant leadership that behooves each one to teach one; to reach towards the rear to help others advance is the generational trust upon which a legacy of greatness rests not only for our next of kin, but also for our kinsman of cultural heritage–the family of Black men throughout the diaspora. It is a precious gift to which we have all been entrusted.

Eric O. Brown

Accountability

I had to start by commending those who have been bold to write about their experiences in life. I did not realize it was one thing to narrate your life experience and another to write about it. I was one of those students in a group assignment who would present the information when the others had completed the work because I didn't like to write, so this, I knew, was going to be challenging; however, I have been excited to share my experiences on this topic knowing that it could also change someone's life.

I define accountability as accepting responsibility for what I said I will do. As I look back at my life, I tried to think back at when I was accountable to myself. This moment took me back to my younger days when I would promise my parents that I would complete my homework but some days not actually do it. There were consequences for not completing that homework, so I learned early that accountability was not just about doing what I said I would do but that there were consequences for not following through. As a child, with what I could understand about being accountable, I didn't take it as seriously as I do now as an adult. When I was a child, my parents were accountable to me in terms of the promise that they would do everything they possibly could to put a roof over our heads, food on the table, ensure that we could be clothed, and also have the best education possible.

Now, as an adult with a family of my own, I have expanded the definition of accountability to include that there are major consequences for the decisions I make whether good or bad. Being accountable as a Black man, a husband, a father and a positive role model is not easy. Society has created a perception that the Black man is not the head of the household and therefore doesn't have anyone to be accountable to. But I choose to not let society define me. I have also taken up the charge to change the perception of the Black family man. Being accountable means ensuring that my family is living comfortably, so whatever I have to do (legally) to provide this care I will do. Every day that I wake up, I ask myself if I did what I intended to do yesterday to live up to this level of accountability. It also means being accountable to my wife and the vows I spoke to her on our wedding day. Most importantly, it means being a role model for my two daughters who look up to me so that they will also follow in my footsteps one day.

···◆◆◆···

Let's take a look at how you can hold yourself accountable. I encourage you to write down your actionable goals. As my mentor used to say, "A goal without a plan is just a wish." This is important because you now have something to work with. If you're just going around saying I'm going to do this or that without any plan, you're not going anywhere. Next, put action steps that describe how your goals will be accomplished next to each goal. Third, determine how you will keep yourself accountable; how you will evaluate yourself against what you said you would do. I would even recommend looking for an accountability partner–maybe someone with the same goals as you. If you have similar goals, you can challenge each other to execute. If you can't find an accountability partner, you may have to find a coach or a mentor. A mentor is someone who voluntarily agrees to assist you by providing guidance and holding you accountable. A coach, on the other hand, is a professional whom you may have to pay for this support; which is fine as long as you have someone holding you accountable.

I remember when I became a real estate agent and had the responsibility of generating my own income. The first year was a difficult time in my life because I had to hold myself accountable. I didn't have a boss or manager that I was accountable to. I had to plan my day and at the end of the day, I had to answer myself about whether I accomplished what I had set out to do. In hindsight, I think I was much more disciplined then because I knew in order to be successful in the business, I needed to complete every task that I set out to do daily, and it paid off. In my second year, I had gotten comfortable and was not accountable to myself, which started to affect my business. So, I had to decide whether I would continue doing what I had been doing and not getting any results or if I would get the accountability I needed to achieve my goals. I decided on the second option and hired a coach, which ended up being the right and best decision. The coach not only got me back on track but also held me accountable for everything I said I was going to do. Some of the questions my coach would ask were what my goals were for the prior week/month and did I achieve them. If I didn't achieve them, she wanted to know the reason and what I had done to correct it. I noticed that those accountability calls with her caused me to think differently and have helped shape my life up to this point.

We are imperfect beings and sometimes we need extra support to get us back on track. That is why I was excited about this book. Black men coming together to share their experiences and life lessons to help other brothers succeed. I hope you've gotten one thing from this book that when applied will make a difference in your life.

Melvin Sarpey

Strength

Strength is an obvious physical attribute that can be readily displayed. We see examples of it each and every day as we look at movies and enjoy our favorite action heroes, see individuals lifting weights or running long distances, observe fitness competitions such as CrossFit®, or soldiers doing pushups. The examples are endless. I would like to believe that everyone possesses some form of physical strength. Variable as it may be, strength is defined in Merriam-Webster dictionary as the *"capacity for exertion or endurance: the quality or state of being strong."[4]*

I would venture to delve deeper into the meaning of strength as a Black man because strength comes in many other forms besides physicality. As you know, our story starts on the foundation of being kings and having dominion over our kingdoms in Africa. We enjoyed Mother Earth's natural resources, the beauty of the plants and animals around us, the abundance yielded by agriculture, the vibrance of the sun, the moon and the stars, differing cultures, languages, and customs, the unity of our families, technological advancements, and prosperity. Our rich story does not start with being enslaved, but we have been persuaded and, at times, forced to have the narrow viewpoint of being monolithic. My brothers, we are so much more than that. Physical and emotional strength resulting from trauma was displayed in the 16th and 17th centuries when we were torn from our land and our families. We have traveled across the expanse of the Atlantic Ocean during the Middle Passage, displaying at every turn, the defined physical and emotional strength of the lion. Clearly, this is a strength like no other. I implore you to learn everything you can about where we have come from, where we have been, and where we are going because here we stand today after arriving on these foreign shores.

My brothers, synonymous with the word strength is *toughness, solidity, and impregnability.*[4] In easier words to understand, strength, and more specifically, Black man strength, is *the power to resist force, the power of resisting attack.*[4] But these definitions can easily become quickly one-dimensional and ill-defining as it relates to the Black male experience. Let us be clear, as Black men, there will be times when you will have failures, experience emotions that will lead you and those around you to tears or you will feel the tremendous weight and anxiety of not being able to accomplish a task set before you. Understand that this is the definition of strength unaccounted for by the dictionary. Rather than being seen as moments of weakness, these very difficult and emotion-provoking moments are an integral part of shaping who you will ultimately become. Strength comes in so many different forms. The strength to endure emotionally and spiritually is equally as important and powerful as the image of physical strength. Furthermore, we should not be afraid to discuss these moments with others and learn from them. Avoid bottling up your emotions. Life will repeatedly present you with challenges and obstacles to impede your progress during your journey. Ultimately, it is how one responds during these difficulties that will help to define your ability to show all forms of strength. Not having the ability to overcome one's obstacles does not mean you are not strong. Contrary to that sentiment is the fact that continuing to fight through adversity shows that you are.

There aren't enough pages to show you examples of Black strength. I encourage you to read and educate yourselves on our proud legacy… Mansa Musa, Amenhotep III, Oba Ewuare, Sonni Ali, the Middle Passage, Jamestown and slavery, Nat Turner, Crispus Attacks, the Great Migration, the role of Black Civil War soldiers, Martin, Malcolm, Treyvon Martin, Michael Brown, and Tamir Rice. Additionally, the Tuskegee Airmen, the Harlem Hellfighters, Nathan Hale Williams, Charles Drew, John Lewis, Muhammad Ali, Lew Alcindor, the 13th Amendment to the U.S. Constitution and victims of mass incarceration, Jesse Jackson, and Barack Obama. Equally important are those who serve the public daily: civil rights organizers, voters, protestors, educators, students, and workers. These are but a few examples of the ups and downs of the Black experience and the manifestation of strength–emotional, political, social, spiritual, and physical. As a people, we have excelled in every field of human endeavor. Don't ever forget that. The point that I am trying to convey to you is to stand up each and every day and take on the world around you as it comes your way. Take a look in the mirror. You are the embodiment of the hope and dreams of kings. Demonstrate strength, my brothers. Embrace it, and never let anyone tell you that you are not strong. Just have an inner or outward talk with yourself—whether it is at home, in school, the workplace, or during your daily interactions. We are strength personified. Together we will go very far as we are our brother's keeper. Seeing the world through the eyes of our ancestors, you just might realize that you are much stronger than you think.

Steven A. Johnson, MD, FACS

Protector

It is inherent for me to be a protector. I am a husband, a father of six daughters, and a son (nephew). There has never been a doubt in their minds as to the extent that I will go to protect them. This confidence that they have in me to protect them is not based on my ability and willingness to protect them physically, but on my ability and willingness to pray for them, provide for them and care for them; as well as lead them, teach them, listen to them, empathize with them, and even give my life for them. The confidence that they have in me is actually in my ability to cover them, and ultimately in my commitment to the responsibility that I have to cover them. As a result of this confidence, they do and always have placed a demand on me to protect them and cover them. This demand is not forced but expected because I have promised them that I would and then I have consistently put forth the effort to do so. As I stay covered, protected, and instructed by spiritual leadership (my pastor), I have promised to do the same for those who come under my responsibility of protection. Being their protector is one of my primary missions in life, and possibly the most important. Covering my family is both my natural and spiritual responsibility. Being their covering is being their protector.

What does this protection look like? Well, as I stated, I have a wife, six daughters, and a son. Being my children's protector started prior to their birth and, in some non-biological instances, upon me assuming the responsibility of being their father. The responsibility of protection includes, but is not limited to, nurturing, teaching, instructing, listening, encouraging, disciplining, demanding, apologizing, and learning. All of these elements of protection fit jointly together but are distinctly separate. None of them are in full operation without the other, but neither of them can replace another. It's imperative to always be conscious of your responsibility (or in this case, I might say position) and its propensity to evolve. Responsibilities don't change, but positions do. For example, you will start to teach less and listen more. You may instruct less and observe more. Or you may even demand less and empathize more. What comes to mind is that they can only learn so much from the passenger's seat. Eventually, you have to put them in the driver's seat. This doesn't lessen your responsibility as their protector, it increases it. There will be situation after situation where these cases arise. To cover and protect properly you must have insight and foresight and be prepared because playing catch up can be costly. One of the best means of preparation for evolving situations is communication–between the parent and child and between both parents (and/or spouse). Communication teaches us about each other and allows us to see into one another. This will in turn build trust.

Do I protect or cover them forever? I am my wife's protector and covering forever! The rest of the clan; definitely not. I am my daughters' covering until I relinquish my authority to their husbands; their new protector. Similarly, I relinquish my authority over my son. I withdraw my position as his covering when he takes on the responsibility of being a covering to his wife. In both cases, I must acknowledge that there is a new dynamic taking place, but I will always be the Fatherly Paraclete. They must always honor me (Ephesians 6:2 NKJV) but are no longer required to obey me. This may sound controversial, but if they maintain their honor for me and I maintain respect for their new protector and covering, their obedience to me will never be an issue. It is very evident that this exchange is not to be taken lightly.

Who qualifies as my replacement covering? You must qualify according to the prerequisites I establish to take responsibility for my daughter. And, just as a gentleman must qualify for my daughter, my son must qualify for your daughter. My pre-requisites are reflective of the Word of God. Physical stature, educational accomplishments, and of course a financial head-start are welcome, but they are not qualifiers. You must match up to what God's word says you must be and I must know that you will cover them as I have. I have been far more than enough, but far less than perfect. Therefore, my requirements are stringent but reasonable; high but attainable.

I believe that my performance as their protector over the last 20 to 30 years has a lot to do with the success or lack of success of their marriages. Being my wife's protector starts with loving her as God loved the church and if necessary, giving my life for her. That's not a cliche and it has many parts to it. Again, pro-tecting her physically is just one part of it. I must protect her by leading her. I lead her not because she is inferior or weak (she is not), but because I am the leader of my home as authorized and ordained by God. I must make sure that I cover her and provide for her amply, not minimally because God entrusted her to me and His supply is definitely more than ample (Ephesians 3:20 NKJV). I must protect my wife by being empathetic to her. I must know her needs, wants, and desires, and aim to exceed them, not just meet them. I must listen to her so that I can provide the necessary support in her areas of need and deficiencies. I must also listen so that I can support her in her areas of strength and gifting. It is necessary to listen in an entirely different way. That is, listen to what she contributes to herself and to me as well as to the family. After all, she has equal and parallel authority and responsibility.

All of the aforementioned depends on my willingness and my ability to hear from God. How do I do this? I must first know what He said in His word (the Bible). I must avail myself to reading and studying the Bible. I must get an understanding (Proverbs 3:5, 4:7 NKJV) of how God protects and how He expects me to protect. The Bible has clear instructions on what the qualifications are to be a husband and father. It has clear instructions on the responsibilities of a husband to his wife (Colossians 3:19, Ephesians 5:25 NKJV) and as a father (Psalm 127:3-5 NKJV). It also has clear instructions on what the wife's responsibilities are to her husband (1 Peter 3:1-6, Ephesians 5:22-24 NKJV) and the children's responsibilities are to their father (Ephesians 6:1-4 NKJV).

···✦✦✦···

As I close, I want to provide you with specific and demonstrable ways in which you can protect your wife and children on a daily basis.

Your wife:

1. Love
2. Respect
3. Spiritual Leadership
4. Attention
5. Devotion
6. Enjoyment
7. Security

Your children:

1. Quality Time
2. Good Communication
3. Discipline
4. Commendation
5. Love and Respect for Their Mother
6. An Example of Godliness
7. Direction

Committing to live out these principles as a way of life will ensure that your family is protected, that your sons are prepared to protect their families, and that your daughters know how to recognize whether a suitor is prepared to protect her.

Barry Ford

Provider

I believe that a man is a direct reflection of the men who raised him. The strengths of a young man's provider will be that young man's strengths and the weaknesses of a young man's provider will be his weaknesses unless he chooses to ground himself and address his weak areas. If you are reading this letter, you are already taking a step in the right direction.

There are many different ways to be a provider. A majority of people are familiar with financial providers but very few are aware of the benefits of having and becoming an intellectual provider. A man's ability to provide should be judged by the contents of his intellect and not solely the depth of his pockets. An easier way to digest and understand that sentence is to compare it to the quote: "Give a man a fish, and you feed him for a day. Teach a man to fish, and you feed him for a lifetime." Remember, earlier I said that a man is a direct reflection of the men around him.

The men around me are not only educated but intelligent. I thank my father for every accolade and award I have earned to date. The principles of living that he has instilled in me, and continues to instill in me, are the reason I can write this letter to you today. (Coincidently, he is the one who notified me about this project and made sure I contributed and followed through with it.) I know that I am one of the few fortunate ones that don't have to look outside of my household for a supportive father figure, and for that I am thankful.

I have decided to devote my life to being an intellectual provider in order to help guide and mold the people in my circle of influence. However, I also believe that he who is the smartest in the room is in the wrong room. Let me elaborate on that for you. The man who finds himself in a situation where he is giving but cannot gain anything from that relationship or group of peers is in the wrong situation. He would be better served to surround himself with those with whom he can equally exchange giving and gaining knowledge and wisdom. No matter how small or large the pieces of information are, in order to become a great provider you must surround yourself with others who will not only sharpen you but challenge you to become a better version of who you are.

···◆◆◆···

I like money. Do you like money? Of course, you do. I have learned that providers must manage money effectively. Interesting factoid: About 2% of the nation's Black dollars are re-circulated in the Black community. The folks over at blackstarproject.org did the math and found that this statistic correlated the length of time a black-earned dollar bill stays in the black community—a staggeringly low six hours.[5]

Back to the point of this letter. Until I got a job and paid my first round of taxes, I undervalued the power of a dollar. I was all too content with texting or calling my mother and father when

I needed financial support. During my childhood and into my teenage years I had the "money grows on trees" mindset. My biggest regret is waiting until I was 18 years old to start learning about money and investing time into understanding finances. As a 20-year-old, I have made leaps and bounds toward securing financial stability and I can only imagine the possibilities that lie ahead.

Let's talk about how I have started to set myself up for the unknown future. One of my goals in 2020 was to open up a separate savings account that I could not access unless I was physically present in a bank. I did this to create a barrier that older generations didn't need to create. Thanks to technology, we now have the option to move, send, deposit, and withdraw money from any account that we own 24/7, 365 days of the year. Knowing that I have compulsive spending challenges, I needed that barrier to prevent me from spending the money in my savings. The second goal I set was to secure another stream of income. For my birthday, I organized a crowdfunding campaign to invest in my technology solutions company, Pair Tech. With the donations, I was able to form an LLC and offer my services to a bigger audience. My third goal was to cut an expense that had been a major part of my budget over the years. My first creative passion was photography and any photographer knows that equipment is expensive. Despite my passion for it, I wasn't producing enough commission work to keep spending 25% of my annual income on it. The fourth and final goal I set was to invest in my primary source of income. I am a Nationally Registered Emergency Medical Technician (NREMT for short). It was time to renew my certification by taking additional training courses. By renewing my national board certification, I could continue to do the life-saving work I love and earn more money while doing so.

These four goals were put in place to set me up financially for the next five years. Every five years I look to evaluate my finances–build income and cut out unnecessary expenditures. I will continue to do this throughout my life to ensure that no matter what the economy does, I will be able to provide for myself and others who may depend on me.

All my life, I was taught that the goal at the end of my metaphorical "day" should be to have options. Having options could be something as simple as being able to set spontaneous dinner dates with friends or being able to make a quick run to the grocery store to try out that new recipe you saw online that day. On the other end of the options spectrum, you may want to have the option to pick between your brand new car and your brand new truck to drive to your office that day. To each his own in how you apply this lesson to your life. For me, securing a career in the high-demand field of healthcare was the first step I took to make sure that I had options. I suggest that you make a list of goals you want to complete in your lifetime, then focus your energy around achieving those goals.

I say all this to convey that when it comes to being a provider, money isn't everything. You should seek to become a well rounded, educated, intellectual provider with financial options that can sustain you and those who depend on you for a lifetime.

Aaron Pair

REFLECT
RIGHTEOUSNESS

"I am convinced that... in the struggle for righteousness, man has cosmic companionship."

Martin Luther King, Jr.

Reflect Godliness

"I'm starting with the man in the mirror. I'm asking him to change his ways. No message could have been any clearer. If you want to make the world a better place, take a look at yourself, and make a change."[6] In Michael Jackson's song, *Man in the Mirror,* these lyrics spoke volumes in how he looked upon his own reflection and realized how he not only affects himself but impacts the world around him.

Now, while Michael's message is charged with a heartfelt battle cry that leaves no doubt of his willingness to take the bull by the horns in his effort to improve himself, the question must be asked… is it enough? Is it enough to look at oneself with a deep introspection or self-examination and create the needed change that not only transforms self but revolutionizes others? I believe he stopped very short at self and did not extend into the idea of existential contemplation. The truth is, we have no ability on our own to produce the highest quality shine without understanding fully our need for God. The house that Jack built—or any name you want to use to fill in the blank—comes with a blaring issue. What you build on your own will require you to maintain on your own. You must have a Godly reflection in order to even see clearly and accurately the man in the mirror.

"In the beginning, God created..." (Genesis 1:1 NIV) "Then God said, 'Let Us make man in Our image'" (Genesis 1:26 NIV). This implies that man has been fashioned and molded as the external and expressed representation of the Eternal swathed in earth and bone. The Maker of Men chose to bless and bestow His creational work with the requisite and compulsion to walk in the light, to be the light, to share the light, and to enlighten others with the light; this is what it means to reflect Godliness.

This visual echo is the greatest indicator in identifying God's plan for mankind and His desire to collaborate with His creation. Godly reflection is the transference of His marvelous light resonating through our inner and outer man, showing itself to be the driving, captivating, and effervescent force from which our finest hours, moments, and accomplishments derive. God's plan is clear-cut and precise in its design and delivery.

Thus, the first step in reflecting Godliness is to grab a hold of God's eternal and unchanging hand, and once you have been secured in His grip, never let go! Hold tight to the light that you will need day to day as God directs and guides your path. See the light, walk in the light, absorb the light, and reflect the light as you see His unending power illuminate your way and your destiny.

"The sun will no more be your light by day, nor will the brightness of the moon shine on you, for the Lord will be your everlasting light, and your God will be your glory. Your sun will never set again, and your moon will wane no more; the Lord will be your everlasting light, and your days of sorrow will end" (Isaiah 60:19-20 NIV).

The second step in reflecting Godliness is to put the reflection on and wear it each and every day. Men spend so much time perfecting the condition of the outer shine (the external man) but give little attention to the internal man. You cannot reflect what you are not in God's eyes. Men, you must be what and who He says you are, not what you say you are! God is not the author of confusion! Be like Adam. Be God's man! (אָדָם Hebrew 'āḏām meaning "man."[7]) Reflect His creation which was made in His image! "So, God created man in His own image, in the image of God created He him; male and female created He them" (Genesis 1:27 NIV). God is very distinct in His creation work. Don't attempt to define or live it as anything else! Whatever form of prayer or devotion inspires you, offer up your supplication daily. Become infilled with the reflection by seeking out the reflection.

Thirdly, own the Godly reflection. Practice wearing and caring for it. Give it daily maintenance. What good is a flashlight if the batteries have lost their strength? It is not the experiences that define our shine. It is the journey… the day to day grind. Emmit Smith said it best, "all men are created equal, but some train harder in the off-season." I'm also reminded of my favorite Mike Tyson quote. He was once asked why he runs and trains at 3:00 am every morning. He replied, "because I know the other guy isn't." Living out those mindsets will cause you to press harder in your need to house a greater reflection of Godliness and to always shine brightly whether you reach your pinnacle or hit your low point. Missing the mark does not always equate to failure, but dark times often shed light on the pitfalls that we may not have seen the last time around. Reflecting Godliness is not always realized when we have our hand raised in victory, but rather when we must get up off the seat of our pants after being knocked down. His reflection in men is built over time by way of consistent living and a will to want His best resonating from within.

Finally, the test. How does one know when he has been effective in reflecting Godliness? There are two ways. People will know who you are and whose you are by the fruit you consistently produce throughout every facet of your existence. That fruit being faithfulness, gentleness, goodness, joy, kindness, long-suffering, love, peace, and self-control (Galatians 5:22-23 NIV). Yes, you are what you eat! Eat Godly light, reflect Godly attributes and watch your garden grow. Secondly, and most importantly, others will benefit from your reflection.

Photosynthesis is the process by which green plants and other organisms use sunlight to synthesize foods from carbon dioxide and water. If your vision or pursuits are not, directly and indirectly, causing other plant life (*people*) to stretch, grow and thrive, you are more than likely reflecting your own personal, self-directed desires, not His Godliness. Yes, you are entitled to attempt to power your tower minus the shower of God's light (*His glory*) with your self-produced lighting; however, just as a plant without sufficient light withers and dies, so too does a man's spirit without His empowerment.

In all that men do; God must be first... not second... not third... but first! He made it plain about reflecting Godliness when He said, "If I be lifted up from the earth, I will draw all men unto me" (John 12:32 NIV). Simply put, reflect Godliness and watch God's glory shine in you, on you, and from you as you gaze on the man that He created in the mirror!

Anthony Mapp

Demonstrate Strong Character

How do you define "strong character?" What does it mean to you personally? I describe strong character as an intentional demonstration of integrity in all one thinks and does. Said differently: consistently striving to do what's right whether someone is observing or not. For instance, strong character is exhibited by the man who sees a person drop a $100 bill when no one–including the person who dropped it–witnessed the event, but picks it up and returns it to the person. Or the woman who promises a starving stranger she will return with food after she has had the opportunity to purchase it and actually keeps her promise. Some examples of strong character are void of money: 1) An uncle showing up for all of his nephew's football games for the season because he said he would, 2) The engineer constantly seeking to give 100% of their effort to every design regardless of the scope of the project, 3) That soldier who provides the ultimate sacrifice through shielding his platoon with his body from a grenade, 4) A teenager deciding to attend school when her close friends are pressuring her to skip class and hang out, and 5) The lawyer who failed the bar exam twice and perseveres to successfully pass on the third attempt.

I believe strong character provides the foundation for the pursuit of righteousness. Before exploring or expounding upon that statement, it is important to share my view of the term "righteousness" to ensure we are communicating with a shared understanding. In a word, I would describe righteousness as perfection. Expressed another way, righteousness is always doing the right thing the right way at the right time no matter the circumstances or environment.

Now that you have heard my perspective on the term righteousness, let us revisit the notion of a strong character providing the foundation for the pursuit of righteousness. Notice the usage of the phrase "for the pursuit of righteousness." I use this phrase because it is my personal belief no human being will ever achieve righteousness in every action or endeavor. To do so, one would achieve a life of perfection which is impossible. However, I also believe we all should aim for righteousness in all we do because this type of behavior leads us to continuous improvement and constant development of its foundation: strong character.

So, what are some ways to develop this foundation of strong character to help us better reflect righteousness? A starting point would be identifying or creating your personal set of core values. For instance, my core values are encapsulated in the following: ensure all my activities are legal, ethical and moral. Let's pause again to create more shared understanding. "Legal" is usually perceived as a straightforward definition with regard to the activity being in the confines of the law or the "spirit of the law." However, the lines of differentiation may be hazy when it comes to "ethical" and "moral." These terms are frequently viewed as synonymous or the same, which they can be at times; however, there is a fundamental difference between the two. My thoughts on the difference between them align with the following description, "Ethical are those codes of conduct that are dictated by the society. However, they may still be immoral for people at a deeper level where his personal belief system resides. Personal belief systems are referred to as morals. These differ from one individual to another."[8] It is paramount to both identify your core values and clearly define them to build strong character, hence the logic supporting articulation of my core values as a basis for this discussion.

Now, back to how I typically use core values to exude strong character. If I am concerned that my thoughts or behavior are not aligned with what I consider strong character, I ask myself the question: Is the action I'm pondering–or in the process of doing–legal, ethical and moral? If the answer is yes, I continue. If it is no, I reevaluate my plan or current actions and strive to make adjustments accordingly. Do I always succeed in "course correction?" No. But I also remember to give myself some grace which is another way of saying I remember to love myself. I think this grace/self-love is a key component to building a strong character because I believe we must first learn to love ourselves before we are able to demonstrate the same to others.

Another key component to building a foundation of strong character is the intentional development of perseverance. I define perseverance as never giving up on a worthy goal. Moreover, perseverance means if one method or technique does not lead one to their specified objective, it is okay and actually a good thing because he knows that particular method or technique does not facilitate achievement of the specified goal. This discovery alerts him to approach the challenge with a different methodology to come a step closer to goal attainment which is undoubtedly progress. For instance, consider the example mentioned earlier of the lawyer who failed the bar exam twice and went on to pass after the third attempt. He continued to pursue the success of passing the bar exam through perseverance or changing his methodology whether that be studying a different way, in a different setting, for different periods of time, or studying different material. One must possess "stick-to-it-ive-ness" or perseverance to consistently align with their core values to cultivate a strong character that leads him on the path to righteousness.

In conclusion, strong character is an intentional demonstration of integrity in all one thinks and does or consistently striving to do what's right whether someone is observing or not. Strong character provides the foundation for the pursuit of righteousness and we all should aim for righteousness in all we do because this type of behavior leads us down the path of continuous improvement. Righteousness in all actions is unachievable so we must allow ourselves some grace or self-love when we miss the mark. Other key components in developing strong character are perseverance and identifying a clearly defined personal set of core values. When we combine these key elements together consistently, we get closer to possessing strong character and exhibiting righteousness.

Lamont Hale

Manage Your Attitude

I am sharing three lessons that have helped me develop a winning mindset. Each has elevated my attitude and strategy towards all things possible in life.

Lesson 1: You are Born a Chooser

In 2007, I was principal of a middle school in Washington, DC. We had a student assembly that featured World Champion Los Angeles Laker and University of Maryland basketball great, Adrian Branch. His message was about the importance of making good choices. Little did I know that a piece of his message would stick with me for years to come. He said to the student body, "You're not born a winner or loser. You are born a chooser."

What Mr. Branch made clear was that winning in life is a choice. What a powerful lesson for us all, young and old. It speaks to the power of our choices. Whether your choices involve passing or failing in school, improving your health, choosing a mate, avoiding destructive behaviors, or helping others, we hold the power to choose the outcomes we want. I'm not suggesting that making the right choice is all we have to do, or that it's easy to choose to do the right thing. What I am suggesting is that being a winner is intentional. You must decide, expect, and plan in order to consistently win.

Lesson 2: Winners Practice

Have you ever played an instrument or learned a second language? We all have learned to walk, then run. Learning anything takes practice and we've had to learn everything we know. There is a point when learning something new becomes comfortable and seemingly automatic. Before we reach that point, the practice required to learn can be difficult.

Not only is life a challenge, but it's also a competition. Like sports, competitions have winners and losers. What drives winners to win? What's unique about their thoughts, behaviors, routines, and habits? One answer is that winners have mastered the art of practice. In practice, you learn, think, and do with coaching, simulation, and repetition. In competition, you rely only on your practiced skills and ability.

The legendary coach of the Georgetown Hoyas, the late John Thompson, spoke on the importance of practice. He compared his coaching to directing a play. He said, "I'm going to pick the script, and I'm going to give them their roles. They're the actors. Their job is to learn those roles–that's what practice is about."

Practice leads to mastery–a key ingredient to winning. We excel at that which we practice; and the more we practice, the more we improve. This is why winning is a habit. It doesn't mean you will always win but if you consistently apply the proper disciplines of practice, you will consistently enjoy the spoils of victory.

Lesson 3: Winning Requires Courage

Courage is the ability to do that which frightens others. It is believed that your heart produces courage. Sports often use metaphors such as "heart of a champion" or "heart of a lion" to describe the courage of winners. Courage gives you an advantage that often separates the victorious from the defeated. Winners leverage their courage.

Mike Tomlin, coach of the Pittsburgh Steelers, led his team to an undefeated start to the 2020 football season. After his team's 10th victory he said, "the only thing perfect about our team is our record." Winning doesn't require perfection, it requires courage–the courage to face the ultimate life challenges with the determination to overcome them.

A courageous decision is one that alters your path in life. I spent much of my adult life on a medically destructive path. I had amassed six chronic illnesses. I had eaten myself into a classification of being morbidly obese with a body mass index (BMI) greater than 50%. Along with that came medical diagnoses of high blood pressure, type 2 diabetes, gout, osteoarthritis, high cholesterol, and sleep apnea. I likened my condition to playing Russian roulette with a bullet in each chamber of life's revolver. Any one of them was lethal. An immediate change was needed or the path I was traveling would kill me. I needed to make a courageous decision, one that would drastically change the path of my life.

The courageous decision I made was to win back my health. It's a process! It takes time to undo decades of damage, but I'm committed for the long-term. One of my choices was to adopt a plant-based diet to improve and reverse my chronic illnesses. I am shifting from taking eight pills a day to eating eight plants a day and it's paying off. As a result, at the time of this writing, my BMI has dropped over 10 points, and my weight is down over 80 pounds. I'm off of cholesterol medicine, and my milligram dosage of all three blood pressure pills has been reduced by 50%. Although I have much more work to do to eliminate my chronic conditions, I have made the courageous decision to win. I will win.

In conclusion, as you approach challenges in your life, reflect on these three critical life lessons. Developing a winning mindset is a choice. Developing a winning mindset takes practice. Developing a winning mindset requires courage. Applying these lessons at any stage of your life will elevate your attitude and enhance your winning mindset. Men, I leave you with the same message as Adrian Branch left with me in 2007, "In all that you do, choose to win!"

H. Eugene L. Pair

Embrace Wisdom

The Bible has hundreds of verses on the subject of wisdom. Thus embracing wisdom and all that it offers can lead you towards a successful and happy life. First, let's start by defining what wisdom is: it is the ability to think and act using personal experiences, insight, common sense, and knowledge. Whereas knowledge is merely knowing something, wisdom uses that knowledge to make the right decisions to reduce the chances of failure.

Over our lifetime, wisdom can be gained from many sources. One source is from trusting relationships. Many of us can think back over our lives and quickly identify the people we trust. That trust was never just given but was earned and developed over time. There was a genuine interest in building you up as a person, young or old, during the trust-building stage. Information on how to be a man, treat people, become successful, and the most important aspects of life were all shared by trusted advisors or friends. This trust allows us to both give and receive advice from one another. Over time, we begin to seek "wisdom" from our trusted relationships because we have experience with them and come to understand and respect the insight coming our way.

As you navigate life, you will find that the advice or knowledge you received will serve as a point of wisdom throughout your life. For some of us, this advice pointed out the importance of staying in school. For others, it corrected us when the decisions of our youth put us in the wrong crowd. Interestingly, during our childhood, we were more willing to accept advice from multiple people, and guidance came from all sides. Our parents, siblings, teachers, coaches, and friends all shared or gave us advice and wisdom to help mold our decisions. Some of these suggestions even came from people younger than us. The fascinating thing about wisdom is that there isn't an age requirement for it, for the giver or its receiver. Remember, it's based on experiences. We didn't always accept the advice or the experiences others were trying to share with us during our youth.

Often, we dismissed it because it didn't align with what we were trying to do or accomplish. We didn't even take the time to vet it. However, as we have gotten older and look back at some of our decisions, we can now see, through our own experiences, both good and bad, the wisdom shared with us. How many of us can remember a coach telling us why showing up prepared for practice was essential and how it would translate into being prepared for a job interview or our job? Or the teacher, expressing the importance of speaking clearly or looking someone in the eyes when talking to them. All of these tidbits were nuggets of wisdom that we found to be important later in life. As we have aged, we can now acknowledge what was being shared and often catch ourselves sharing similar wisdom with others.

This realization of wisdom comes from our ability to have thoughtful reflections centered on our lives. Brothers, one of the best ways to embrace wisdom is to look back over your own life and summarize the lessons you've learned over time. These reflections allow us to gather our lives' experiences and start turning the corner to identify our own wisdom. Whether you have reached your dreams or not, you have learned so much over your lifetime. Often, we underestimate the value of our own life experiences and the impact of these experiences. Why do you feel the way you do about life? Why did you choose your career? Why is family so important to you? As men, we tend to shy away from self-reflection. However, this awareness and knowledge should be gathered and shared with others when opportunities exist to do so. We must be willing to learn from one another's experiences and look for opportunities to pass this wisdom along. For example, for those men who grew up in the inner city and have made it out of "public housing" or "the projects," your experiences, knowledge, and insight are valuable to young men still in that situation. You're an example of not only making it out but what it took to do it. Or for those men of color who had to navigate the isolation of the corporate boardroom, your experiences and the knowledge gained over the years are valuable to those coming behind you. Just like its definition, wisdom provides insight.

When I was a teenager, my father taught me a precious lesson about wisdom. I honestly didn't understand its value until I became an adult, but now, I share the lesson with as many people as possible. The lesson centered on people who were less fortunate than me. He told me, "When you see a bum on the street, don't judge them or make assumptions. Some of them may have been very rich at one time. Instead of walking by them like they don't exist, buy them a cup of coffee and ask them how they ended up on the street." He explained that they might not be able to help you with what's currently going on in your life, but they may be able to share the decisions they made that put them on the streets, and through their experience, maybe I could avoid the same wrong decision. I've shared this life lesson with the students I've taught, the young men I've coached, and even my son. Wisdom sometimes isn't about how to make it. Quite often, it's learning from the mistakes of others.

The last thought on embracing wisdom I wish to share is on the need for us as Black men to let go of our pride to learn from others. We can no longer stand in place and try to figure it out on our own. We need to realize that when wisdom is being shared, it's a time to just listen. Frequently, we take the long road trip through life, ignoring what others are telling us. We try to skip steps in order to achieve our goals faster. For instance, my favorite discussion with male students who are struggling in school is around following the path. I explain to them that I get their independence. I get their need and determination to rely on themselves. However, what I don't get is the continual denial of what's not working. How many more failures or heartaches must you experience before you reach out for guidance? Why are you choosing to walk through the forest, through the mud, or experience pitfalls before realizing a paved sidewalk is next to you? You see, people have gone before you to create a path for you. They have gained knowledge and survived the pitfalls already. All you have to do is listen to their advice and follow the path laid out for you.

Part of the importance of embracing wisdom is recognizing when wisdom is needed. Brothers, we need to start using all of our experiences to make sound judgments around our decisions. Furthermore, we must be willing to seek knowledge from one another before making a decision. It's time for us to share our experiences with each other to make us all wiser. We should all be looking for ways to share what we know with one another. For example, if you're starting a business, it makes sense to sit down and talk with someone who has a successful business. After that conversation, look for advice from people in the same business sector you want to be in and surround yourself with wiser people than you who are willing to guide you along the way.

As Black men, we should be providing insight for generations both present and to come. See, the thing about wisdom is, it's not designed to be harbored by us individually. It should be embraced by both the giver and the receiver.

O. Michael Edge, Ed.D

Be Humble

To the young Black man starting up the corporate ladder, I am writing to you because I have been you. I have worked in corporate America for over 23 years. I work in an industry where few people at my level look like me and even fewer share my background. An industry where even now, in these "enlightened" post-Obama times, it is considered acceptable to make insensitive comments in a business setting on issues like Black Lives Matter. Sometimes operating in this arena requires aggression, sometimes it requires withdrawal. The way in which you can effectively channel your aggression and activate your withdrawal must be based on your particular style, motivations, and ambitions. But regardless of which course you follow, you will need mindfulness based on mental strength rooted in humility.

I think mental strength that borders on arrogance is an essential tool that a young man should have, especially an ambitious young Black man determined to climb the corporate ladder. Everybody has a beating coming from the realities of life… everybody does. I think the luckiest people have their real-life whippings spread out over their lives, somewhat evenly with occasional crests and dips. Some folks get a huge helping of their beatings early… I am one of those people. I think this potentially traumatic scenario leads to one of two extreme results: a weakling or a warrior. The mental strength I brought into the battlefield helped me develop into the latter.

This mental strength is not the empty "attitude" that masquerades as accomplishment with all too many thought leaders and "influencers." It is a simple and pure belief in yourself and the validity of your ambitions. So much so that your challenges will become stepping stones to where you are headed, never seeming to be impediments. This mental strength will often be perceived as arrogance or aloofness. It will engender respect.

Paradoxically, this mental strength is also rooted in your humility. And by humility, I mean your awareness of your place in relation to the people and structures around you. There are several keys to this humble awareness. They include:

1. Your understanding that in order to achieve you will have to buckle down and hone your craft because you will often have to be better than everyone else to be deemed their equal. This is not glamorous. You might not be considered the "next big thing." You will be stronger for it when the dust settles, the glamour fades, and you are found to be the best-armed warrior in the field.

2. Your acceptance of the fact that if you are not failing, you are not trying, and that there are only 12 inches between a pat on the back and a kick up the rear end. It takes humility to be hit in the mouth with a learning

curve, low expectations from society, and the fact that sometimes the people who should be supporting you do not expect much from you. It takes mental strength rooted in this humility to absorb the hits, dust yourself off, and keep moving forward.

3. Your freedom from a fear of admitting ignorance, because in your humility you accept that you do not know everything. And in your arrogance, you learn not to care about the opinions of others. Remember, you're only ignorant until you've asked the question. (Funny thing is, you will often find that people were faking insight until you asked!)

4. Your awareness of the fact that defining yourself by your job leads to certain disappointment and possible self-destruction (unless you're the boss, then it's likely but not certain). Also, your awareness that you can easily be replaced and it might have nothing to do with your job performance. So, it is as important to ensure that your job meets your goals as it is to ensure that you measure up to your employer's expectations.

5. Your acknowledgment of the fact that your job can go on without you and it is essential to build a vibrant and active personal life and maintain a work/life synergy. Your personal headspace is sacred and essential (I operate a graphic arts business on the side for this very reason).

I hope I have made you aware of the humility needed to thrive as a young Black rookie in the corporate world while emphasizing the need to build up the emotional fortitude that is needed to armor yourself against the challenges to come. I will not lie, there will be times when your resolve will be tested. Unconscious bias is REAL and you will need the arrogance to stare it down coupled with the humility to analyze and overcome any obstacles that you encounter. I wish you strength, health, and all the luck in the world as you face the challenges coming your way.

Roger Okewole

Grow Your Mentality

"For as he thinks in his heart, so is he…"

Proverbs 23:7 (NKJV)

A male baby grows into a toddler, a toddler into a young boy, a boy into an adolescent, and an adolescent into a man. This natural progression, marked by the manifestation of physical characteristics associated with manhood, largely occurs biologically and autonomously through the release of hormones in accordance with the master creator's grand design. Society has long identified that the same baby assumes the benefits and burdens of "manhood" at 18 years of age. But society's rote bestowment of manhood at the age of 18 is deceptive. In fact, the better measure of manhood is not through the mere passage of time and the physical manifestation of stereotypical physical characteristics, but instead via an assessment of and commitment to the strength of one's mindset.

The world sees our physical presentation. How we dress. The words we say. The work we do (and how we do it). These actions also become the conduits for the display of our emotions–i.e. how we feel about any given matter manifested through these actions. Importantly, we rarely distinguish between the way we feel and the way we think–but that is a critical distinction for a man to understand. In other words, your emotions and thoughts are two separate functions of your existence. One can feel disappointed about not receiving a promotion but think that it is best to maintain a professional demeanor regarding the decision. The mind is the control center for all of these things–how you process the occurrence and the discipline to manifest behavior notwithstanding how one "feels." While this is counter-intuitive to society's tendency to extol and prioritize feeling in decision-making, it is absolutely essential. The mind is the grand conductor of your existence as a man–and in order to be a highly functioning man, you have to seize control of it, oftentimes subverting emotions that will lead to poor decision making in the process.

Indeed, before success or failure manifests itself in the accomplishment of a result, the progress towards either end is first fashioned in one's mind. How one makes decisions is a function of the information one has; and also, more importantly, the information one does not have! Therefore, one's unintentional ignorance, rooted in a fundamental lack of knowing, can be a devastatingly limiting factor in achieving one's potential. In this time of extraordinary technological advances that have made the wisdom of the ages literally available with an internet connection, the issues that have plagued prior generations who sought to grow their mentality–having access to information–is no longer a legitimate hindrance to developing a growth mindset. The knowledge to improve ourselves is readily available, now more than at any other time in the history of mankind.

But how does a man accomplish this feat of "seizing control" of his mind in order to "grow it." The first step is to commit to shrinking the universe of what you know that you don't know. This can only be accomplished through extensive reading and incorporating the wisdom of those who have accomplished the things that you seek in your heart. So the question then becomes, why don't all men purposefully and regularly engage in this fundamental behavior of stimulating a growth mindset? For some, positive thoughts of achievement, abundance, and success may not come naturally—in fact, it may feel unnatural, phony, and uncomfortable to fashion goals about things coming to pass that neither you nor anyone in your sphere of influence has ever accomplished. However, that feeling is not how a man of any achievement gauges what is worthwhile to pursue. In fact, the presence of discomfort is often a sign of growth. Just as one can expect aching and sore muscles following the initiation of physical exercise in the pursuit of improved physical vitality, one can expect analogous discomfort in the pursuit of a similar development of the mind.

And just as the manner in which the body atrophies from the lack of explicit and targeted cultivation through exercise, the mind similarly must be exercised to both protect and expand beyond one's current ability or skill through concerted daily dedication to improving one's mindset. In fact, the idea of simply maintaining your mindset is a false notion—we are either growing or declining, in all aspects of life.

As we move in the world and connect with a critical mass of men of success and of lesser accomplishment, it becomes clear that the key differentiator in men is not external factors, but rather can be largely attributed to how these men think about themselves and the world. Not their birthplace. Not their race. Not their socio-economic status. What is in their mind is in them. And what is in a man is a result of what was placed in that man—whether by himself or something/someone else. So it is incumbent of all men to be mindful of what has been placed in their mind and what they are currently placing in their mind, and, upon that assessment, get to the business of making the necessary adjustments to accomplish their goals.

Society imposes the identity of "leader" on men as if the genetics of a man alone imbues the individual with the characteristics and traits of leadership. Those who adopt this belief do so at the peril of anyone or anything that they purport to have a sincere interest in leading—whether at home, in the community, or the workplace. Before you can lead anyone else, a man has to first lead himself. And the battle of self-leadership begins in the mind of the man. The extent to which one is successful in becoming better in any role that he plays in society is in direct proportion to the commitment that man has to growing his mindset.

Wali W. Rushdan II, Esq.

Foster Righteous Relationships

"My dear brothers and sisters, take note of this: Everyone should be quick to listen, slow to speak and slow to become angry, because human anger does not produce the righteousness that God desires."

James 1:19-20 (NIV)

I believe the above scripture, regardless of your faith or belief system, encompasses the necessary tools to cultivate righteous relationships as we continue to move and grow in this world. Many industry leaders and scholars have suggested that we have recently transitioned into the fifth industrial revolution where humans and machines are learning to dance with one another. Therefore, as the world continues to change and evolve with new technology and artificial intelligence, it is paramount as men that we develop the necessary skills to nurture righteous relationships at every stage of development because authentic human connection will prove to be more valuable than ever.

When thinking about this topic I often thought about the quote I read as a history teacher years ago when discussing the Obama family traditions with my classes.

> "One ritual President Obama practiced every night involved leaving work at six-thirty so he could enjoy dinner with his family. He writes: "There was nothing more refreshing than spending that time with the three most important people in my life — listening to Malia and Sasha narrate their days, ask questions and tease me to no end. Afterwards, Michelle and I might get a few extra minutes alone to catch up. I always found myself replenished, as though my family had decluttered my mind and restored my equilibrium."

I juxtapose the above quote with the traditions my late mother instilled in our family at the dinner table. I believe it was the lessons I learned here that helped me nurture personal and professional relationships throughout my life that can be beneficial to everyone.

My mom told me, "mealtime is an ancient family ritual never to be subverted by distractions because people best connect when they eat together." That always resonated with me and with that I want to leave you with the acronym EAT as a reference to help guide you along your journey in cultivating your own righteous relationships.

Engage. Engage with your friends, family, classmates, and colleagues–with your undivided & undistracted attention. Developing fruitful relationships requires us to be fully engaged with the people in our lives from conversations, emails, texts and just being there to support. Engagement requires actively being involved in whatever you choose to become a part of.

Engagement requires putting in that sweat equity with both kind words and actions. For example, Civil Rights Attorney Bryan Stevenson has been described as having a very empathetic and engaging demeanor necessary for his life work.

Ask. Ask questions, ask for help, ask for guidance, ask for mentorship, ask for constructive criticism from your peers and elders. From my experience, authentic relationships truly develop when people are genuinely curious about other people, their lives, hopes, and dreams. These relationships can be taken to the next level when you make it a practice to listen more than you talk, especially in social gatherings. Make it a practice to genuinely get to know people in your presence by asking them questions. In addition, as relationships continue to flourish and grow, do not hesitate to ask for guidance and mentorship; especially from older people you meet.

It is important that we make and establish lasting relationships with older and more experienced people. I know I greatly benefited from the lasting relationships and mentors I gained through my fraternity when I attended Ohio University. It is also important to establish a diverse network of peers and mentors. Never limit yourself as a byproduct of your environment or opportunity. I often think back to this interview I listened to a year ago about a brain surgeon who came to this country as a migrant laborer.

> "After that, I ended up going to community college and then I met my first mentor, who took me under his wings and began to teach me the ways. But

he was, that's how I got introduced, it was mentor-ship, Michel. It was people who believed in me, but they are not people who looked like me. If I waited for a mentor that looked like me, I would never find one at the time, and probably even now. So you have to look around for people who are good people, and they don't necessarily have to look like you. And that's exactly what got me going from point A to Berkeley, eventually, to Harvard, residency, and now where I am today."[9]

—Dr. Alfredo Quinones-Hinojosa

Trust. Trust is built over time. Righteous relationships are built through bonds of trust and authenticity and the time we put in via our words and actions. People must trust they can count on us to be fully present, involved, and genuinely concerned about their overall well-being. I often think of the African Proverb, "When you pray, move your feet." I believe trust relies heavily on moving your feet and being there for the people and the relationships in your life. As trust is established over the years, the more people you meet and encounter will also trust that you are being your authentic self and relationships will continue to grow.

I will forever hold on to the wisdom my late mom gave me and truly believe she was right in that relationships are cultivated when people EAT together.

Aaron Jeter

BE PROSPEROUS

"Build your own pyramids, write your own hieroglyphs."

Kendrick Lamar

Create Legacy

Negus. That word may elude you but research it, you'll be pleased with what you find. That is why I say our history is so rich that many individuals don't want us to know our roots and oftentimes attempt to take credit for our genius ancestry. I am not here to give you a history lesson but I do implore that you seek knowledge beyond what is given to you. I'm here to share with you about legacy and why we need to be more adamant about making sure as men (the lineage) we do our duty and leave a rich legacy and prepare the next generation. I'm honored to be given the chance to rap with you for a short while. But before we dive in, I have to ask you: What is your legacy? What does the word legacy mean to you? What legacy will you leave?

(Keep these questions in mind as you read.)

Initially, I thought I knew what creating a legacy meant... living a great life, having children, and leaving a massive inheritance for my descendants; and a lot of people would agree.

However, after recently surviving the pandemic of 2020 and several unforeseen life-changing circumstances because of it; I now have a different perspective on life. I thought one had to live this thing called life perfectly. I was hiding my failures and covering up my weaknesses but now I've realized that perfection is an unachievable misconception of leading a great life. I've learned that the mistakes are what actually make the journey of creating your legacy worthwhile.

When it comes to creating a legacy, the process consists of a few components: passion, impact, and the story but not necessarily in that order.

Your story essentially encompasses the other two components, passion and impact, which tend to come later in life. Nonetheless, from the time you are born until the time you die, you are creating your legacy. We are all striving to make the dash that separates those two dates memorable!

As you are growing up as a young man your parents/family, your environment, your culture, your upbringing/spirituality, and your friends all shape your attitude and actions.

I'll share my story with you as an example. I grew up in a military household (both Navy parents) so we moved quite often. My brother and I had to learn how to make friends quickly but also cope with the fact that we could be moving at any time. Growing up, I took everything at face value simply because my parents were my protection. They were the covering. I trusted them to do things that were in my best interest. So, I adopted their beliefs, customs, values, traditions, and more. It wasn't until I went to college that I truly transitioned into manhood. It was then that I realized that they equipped me with the tools to lead a life worth living and narrate my own story, on my own, as a MAN!

After failing a number of courses, ruining relationships, wrecking a few cars, and even getting fired from my first job out of college my journey got better.

I was able to start my own mentoring program with the field experience I gained over the four years at my job and the branding/marketing experience from working a business with my father.

My story doesn't stop there: The 2020 Pandemic put my mentoring program on pause so I had to diversify my efforts into generating other streams of income. I also experienced a ruptured Achilles tendon which rendered me temporarily immobile. Life doesn't stop because you encounter some hardships. These setbacks are meant to invoke reflection and growth. It requires you to be present, process the situation, confront your weaknesses, manage your emotions, and navigate through the trial. Some may be more difficult than others but the true victory comes with being able to reassure the next man that conquering his hardship is more than feasible and enjoying life after is the reward.

···◆◆◆◆···

Passion? This one is tricky and it's okay if you feel lost because finding your passion feels like wandering around aimlessly in the forest in the pitch black. You don't know where to go, you don't know who to trust but once you find it, it's like having a lantern with an inextinguishable flame. Your passion is the fire that lights your path. I usually ask my mentees what's worth dying for or better yet what's your reason for living.

Your legacy is what you'll be remembered for doing. This was rather difficult for me to navigate because in my early years I wanted to be in the NBA but when that possibility dwindled I was miserable and borderline depressed. I had no desire to push forward or continue college because that was the motivation behind my academic success. I gave basketball so much of my time that I forgot to nurture my other talents like the piano, art, puzzles, poetry, and more.

It's important that you find your inspiration but it's equally as important that you don't allow it to consume you to the point that you lose sight of the other beauties of life. It's also important to find what motivates you outside of your passion, so when times are tough you don't abandon it.

Fortunately for me, I was able to identify a new passion for helping young men and develop that into a business, something I can leave to my children. With this, I can make a positive impact on both my family and the community. You never know how operating within your passion can not only inspire but also unconsciously liberate others to operate within their own.

Finding your passion may not be easy, and it may change but it's imperative to identify it so you can develop your legacy!

···◆◆◆···

If you were to die today what would people say about you? You may have heard this quote from Nipsey Hussle, "The best thing you can do for a person is to inspire them. That's the best currency you can offer: inspiration." Your impact on people plays a huge role in your legacy... because they are the ones that tell your story.

Visualize this for a second: Think about a person you admire and everything you associate with that person. Now, do the same for a person you despise and everything you associate with that person. In less than five minutes you created the narrative for those two people, good or bad, right or wrong, simply based on interactions. These individuals left you with something whether that be physical, emotional, material, or philosophical. Nonetheless, they have impacted your life in a way that you will always remember. This is how others will define you and that will be your legacy!

···✦✦✦···

Are you familiar with the concept of Sankofa? It is the idea that you reach back to gain knowledge and bring it forward to help in the present and that you reach back to help others. I stress Sankofa because I believe each of us has a duty to come back and help out. This is the very reason I and these other distinguished men are writing this book. We understand that we did not achieve the level of success we have through our efforts alone. I understand we can sometimes get lost in the desire for further advancement in life and we may forget to make a conscious effort to reach back. Every so often, ask yourself what you are giving back to your family, your friends, your community. This is where the real work is done. Anyone can become rich and successful but it takes someone special to help others to do the same.

Don't be the individual who is looking for recognition or compensation for any and everything they do. One of my mentors told me this and it stuck with me, "A candle loses nothing by lighting another candle;" which simply means it costs you nothing to genuinely inspire someone else.

···◆◆◆···

As I said before, your legacy consists of a few components: passion, impact, and the story. You may find one before you start to identify the others but just like a recipe, without one of the ingredients, the recipe is incomplete. Take time to develop each component so you can pass down your rich recipe for success!

Your story is never over whether you choose to respect it or neglect it. What you do in your life will either be praised by your descendants as they speak about you around the fire or murmured in dismay and disappointment. So, what history are you writing? What does legacy mean to you? What legacy will you choose to leave?

···◆◆◆···

Here's an activity that can really put things into perspective. Grab a piece of paper and write your eulogy. Write it exactly how you would want to be remembered. Share your story: the glory, the shame, the laughs, and the pain. How did you live out your passion? What did you leave to your loved ones? How did you impact those close to you and the broader community? Once you finish writing it, save it, and start living it. Live out your legacy!

Andre' Valines

Find Your Purpose

Purpose is defined as "the end to which one is striving in life; one's reason or motivation for living."[10] The purpose of this writing is to inspire the life-purpose-seeker in achieving his motivation.

The Bible notes that Mordecai questioned whether Esther had… "come to your royal position for such a time as this?" (Esther 4:14 KJV) It also identifies a poor, wise man who saved the city; but, then was quickly forgotten (Ecclesiastes 9:15 KJV). It also mentions Simon of Cyrene (Matthew 27:32 KJV), a Black man who carried Jesus' cross for possibly a few miles for just a moment in time.

Many believe the biggest thing in your life is your purpose; especially, when it includes millions of dollars. But if so, why didn't Dikembe Mutombo disappear into the shadows after ending his basketball career? Instead, he built a $29,000,000, 300-bed hospital on the outskirts of the Congolese capital of Kinshasa. Why didn't Oprah Winfrey vanish after becoming a millionaire? Instead, she invested $40 million to establish the Oprah Winfrey Leadership Academy for Girls south of Johannesburg, South Africa. Why weren't their lives over? Neither became irrelevant like the poor wise man who saved the city;

whose name is hardly remembered. Or, are Dikembe and Oprah finished? Have they completed their purpose? Can they do something else important? What of Esther or King David who were both notable as teens? Were their lives worthless thereafter? Especially for Esther, of whom we hear nothing else notably achieved after that moment. And what about the old man? The town leaders knew who he was. Thus, he had done some notable acts previously. For Him and King David, which event was their "purpose?" And for each of these people, how did each find purpose?

I propose that purpose is not just one, large, recognizable thing. In John 18:37 (KJV), Jesus said, "...for this cause I have come into the world, that I should bear witness to the truth." I John 3:5 (KJV) says that Jesus "... was manifested to take away our sins," and "For this purpose the Son of God was manifested, that he might destroy the works of the devil (John 3:8 KJV). I John 4:9 (KJV) says, "...God sent His only begotten Son into the world, that we might live through him." And I John 4:10 (KJV) states that "He (God) loved us, and sent his Son to be the propitiation for our sins." All of these are statements of purpose yet they are all very different and still lead to an overarching mission. But the Bible calls all of these statements His purpose (cause, reason sent, or manifested). Thus, purpose can be one, a couple, or many motivations building upon each other, or not. And maybe that depends. Like that idiom, *beauty is in the eye of the beholder.* So how do we answer the questions that many, if not all of us, will ask at some point: God, why am I here? What is my purpose?

In the very beginning (Genesis 1:1-2 KJV), "God created the heaven and the earth. And the earth was without form, and void." In Black's Law Dictionary, *void* is defined as "having no legal force or binding effect, unable, in law, to support the purpose for which it was intended."[11] Thus, was the earth void of purpose?

Well, immediately God begins to declare purpose. He purposes light and darkness to define day and night. God purposes the firmament to divide heaven from earth (Genesis 1:6 KJV). God purposes the land to "bring forth grass, the herb *that* yields seed, *and* the fruit tree *that* yields fruit" (Genesis 1:11 KJV). God purposes the water to abound with creatures (Genesis 1:20 KJV). God purposes the lights and stars (Genesis 1:14-16 KJV). God continues and defines the purpose of man and woman to multiply (Genesis 1:28 KJV). God defines a specific purpose/work for man (Genesis 2:15 KJV) to take care of the earth and tend the Garden of Eden; the woman is his help-mate. Throughout all of God's creation, God identifies a purpose immediately. He gave a general purpose, and often, a specific purpose. Now, Malachi 3:6 (KJV) states "For I am the Lord, I change not." Therefore, please accept that God created you, even these many centuries after creation, with a purpose immediately identified. Therefore, you must find the will of God for your life to find your purpose.

After revealing the general things, with time and searching, God reveals the hidden things (Jeremiah 33:3; I Corinthians 2:7, 14:2 KJV) of your life. He promises. Matthew 6:33 (KJV) says "seek ye first the kingdom of God and His righteousness and all these things shall be added unto you." Proverbs 3:6 (KJV) says, "In all thy ways acknowledge Him, and He shall direct thy paths." And Jeremiah 29:13 (KJV) promises that if you seek God, you will find Him. God wants you to find Him and wants you to fulfill your purpose. Romans 12:2 (NLT) encourages you to "... let God transform you... Then you will learn to know God's will for you." Therefore, if you find God in His word, you will find your purpose.

Reading God's word tunes you to His radio frequency. John 10:4 (KJV) says, "...and His sheep follow Him because they know His voice." But your purpose doesn't just drop into your lap (Deuteronomy 1:8 KJV), for many reasons including your own choices. But God wants you to seek Him seriously. Once you seek God truthfully, Philippians 2:13 (NIV) says, "...for it is God who works in you to will and to act according to His good purpose." And Psalms 32:8 (NLT) states, "I will guide you along the best pathway for your life. I will advise you and watch over you."

Romans 12:6 (KJV) states that each of us has "gifts differing according to the grace that is given to us" by God. Thus, as you seek God and His will, God begins to reveal those hidden things He has placed within you (Jeremiah 33:3 KJV). The drive of what is in you begins to propel you. As the radio frequency gets stronger, you learn more about what you enjoy and your talents, you develop skills, and God opens opportunities and directs you. Often, even when you're not sure you are following correctly, you find He has been leading you all the while.

Skills, likes, talents, experimenting, exploring, trying, failing, training, mistakes, successes, growth, dislikes and living life, all lead to discovering your purpose. There are even times you will discover an ability you flow effortlessly in performing, and even enjoy, while not feeling totally pleased with the results. There are also times, due to God's Holy Spirit, when you know that the time, activity, and/or place is just right for you. You can receive a knowing, a peace, a strength, a knowledge that just feels RIGHT and true, without being able to explain how you know; you simply know. "You shall know the truth, and the truth shall make you free" (John 8:32 KJV). You should make a note of these occurrences as helpful hints toward finding your purpose.

Finding your purpose is about discovering you. It does not include comparing yourself with others but enjoying the journey of discovering. It requires you to take particular notice of yourself, sharing who you are, discovering what's inside of you. This will not only please God; it will also please you. This journey of realization is one God wants to walk hand-in-hand with you. At times you may let go of His hand and run ahead or turn incorrectly. He waits and longs to continue the journey with you.

Purpose has an ebb and a flow. It's not just a destination. Purpose is an adventurous journey of challenges and discoveries of self and relationship with the Creator. It is meant to be enjoyed. God is not disappointed if we shoot for the sun, but land among the stars… if we enjoyed the trip… and shoot again. You see, only God can finish a work and eternally rest. Therefore, the Holy Ghost continues to inspire us toward what God has completed as a portion that we should enjoy.

To find your purpose in life is to pursue life; to live, grow, and expand. Your purpose does not end. It morphs and expands as you live and seek God. How can it end when you are partnered with God? Also, purpose and passion are discovered by engaging people and engaging in the world. Therefore, find a task or problem that engages your creativity, desires, and energies regularly.

As I conclude, know that many people find their purpose and they may not necessarily attribute it to finding God. Purpose, in most cases, is verified from within. But there are two who ultimately decide what an entity's purpose is. The creator of the entity and the user of the entity (if not the entity itself).

Yes, a butter knife spreads butter, but it can be used as a screwdriver. A purpose I may regret if it cuts my hand while turning the screw or if the knife breaks. We are created beings designed with a purpose in mind. But I guess that depends on whether you believe that everything we know was created by the random, multiple tossing up of atoms, elements, etc. Or that we were created by an intelligent being. I expect the Creator to be an intelligent and complicated being.

"Many plans (motivations) are in a man's mind, but it is the Lord's purpose for him that will stand" (Proverbs 19:21 AMP). "The purpose in a man's heart is like deep water, but a man of understanding will draw it out" (Proverbs 20:5 ESV). You don't want to get to the end of life and displease the Creator, lack fulfillment, and miss your purpose(s). Remember, even a broken butter knife can still fulfill its purpose, though it may no longer work with screws.

So, if your handler is the God Jehovah, and you seek Him and trust Him, you will find Him and He will lead you.

OT Stanley

Complete Your Assignment

As Black men, we have an incredible responsibility to aid and assist our youth and even some of the adults in our community. There are many assignments that we will have to participate in over the course of our lives. And when one assignment is over, there is another assignment ready to be tackled.

The first assignment given to us is a commandment written in the Bible: Honor thy mother and father (Ephesians 6:2 NIV). Before you can lead a community, nation, or a team, you must honor your parents. What does that mean? Many of us are born into this world with two people to help guide us from infancy through our adolescent years and into adult life. They have a vested interest in our well-being and imparting wisdom to us; wisdom developed from their time on this earth and the things they have experienced. It is their job to teach us right from wrong, good from bad, how to treat people, how to behave, how to love, how to read... I can go on and on. There are many children who listen to their parents, yet there are many who don't. That is the first test we must pass. Honoring your mother and father simply means respecting them and listening to them, even when you don't agree with them.

When I was a child, my dad would tell me to do certain things that I did not agree with; in fact, at times I argued with him about it. But as I got older, I started to realize that what he was saying was true and that he was only trying to help me. In fact, the older I got the more I realized how wise my father was, and had I just listened to him, I would not have gone through the growing pains I experienced. It wasn't that I never listened to him, but sometimes I was a little headstrong. Unfortunately, growing up I had friends who did not listen to their parents and it did not end up well for them. Some of them ended up in jail, some ended up out of work, in and out of relationships, etc. I can credit listening to my parents most of the time to now being married for 23 years, running a successful business, having three wonderful children in college, and maintaining a great relationship with my parents. I still honor my parents today as a 50-year-old man. Because of my relationship with my parents, my children honor their parents. What I've learned in my short life is that most things are repeated generation after generation after generation, whether good or bad. So, our first assignment, to model the people who are raising us to be good men and women, is simple but critical to our success.

The second assignment is to find a mentor. As we get older and get into our teenage years or move on to college, it is important to seek guidance from people outside of your home; people who you admire or look up to. It could be a coach, an academic adviser, or a teacher–someone who can help point you in the right direction as you move to the next phase of your life. Your parents are important, but they don't know everything. If you are fortunate, they will give you the spiritual base you need and help establish a strong foundation for doing the right things. But they cannot teach you specifics about the career and or business that you want to go into if they don't have that specialized knowledge. It is important to connect with someone you look up to who can assist you in your next phase of life. In my case, it was a college coach. I was fortunate enough to be a college athlete and my coach was very influential in shaping how I see the world. He taught me life principles about finishing what I start, having a strong work ethic, leading by example, having my teammates' backs, and so many more. I was able to take that knowledge and perspective about life into the workforce, apply it, and become very successful. My coach also taught me how to win.

The next assignment is very important for us as Black men. We must lead by example and from the front. If you want something done, you do it. You cook, you clean, you work, you run; you do it first then others will follow. I would never ask my children to do something that I haven't done myself. When you are a leader you take full responsibility for your life. You make no excuses and you take whatever comes with the decisions that you've made. Once you become a leader–leading yourself first and then others–you can create a great life for yourself and your family. However, this is not your final assignment.

Once you've made it, another assignment will be thrust upon you. This assignment is to mentor someone else and help others. We are here on this earth to be of service to our fellow man. Nobody cares what type of car you drive, how big your house is, how many friends you have on social media, etc.

People want to know how you can help them; how can you help humanity. There are so many melanated men and women who need our help. There are gifted children who cannot afford college. There are great athletes in the inner cities who cannot afford shoes to run track or play basketball. There are graduates of colleges who need assistance in finding jobs or just need to be given an opportunity to work at your company. Who have you helped?

I often ask myself, what is my assignment now? Why am I here? It is clear that my assignment now is to help as many people who look like me as possible. If you are reading this book that is your assignment as well... to help as many people as you possibly can, especially those who look like you.

Orin Solomon

Focus on Growth

Beloved brothers, the cornerstone of all your successes will be your ability to consistently focus on your own growth. Before you dismiss this as the same motivational mumble jumble that you have heard before, take a moment to better understand what real growth is and what it is not.

Growth is not about listening to as many podcasts, Ted Talks®, books, CDs, and DVDs that you can get your hands on so that you can go around quoting aphorisms but it is the process of focusing on a concrete plan to improve in a specific area of your life with measurable and demonstrable results. I am convinced that the physical, observable world is a mere lens for us to learn the fundamental truths that apply in the metaphysical world. Everything in nature grows through the same exact process. A tree must absorb minerals from the dirt and light from the sun in order to grow. As babies, we must drink water and eat food in order to grow into men and women. If life is not properly nourished and fed it doesn't reach its full potential; in fact, it will die. As human beings, we cannot survive more than three days without drinking water and three weeks without food. Just as we must continue to nourish our physical bodies to grow, we must nourish our minds with the information and insights needed to grow in the metaphysical world. It is only in rare circumstances that we would even consider going a single day without food or water. We must adopt the same philosophy to not go more than a day without nourishing our minds to grow towards our goals. We must be consistent with our daily intake of information to achieve growth.

···◆◆◆◆····

I started my professional career in a technical role as a business analyst. Although it wasn't what I studied in college, I was able to commit myself to a growth plan so I could learn what was needed to be successful in that role. I set a daily goal to spend time learning a new database language that I ultimately used to improve processing time on my client's project by several days. As a result of the value this brought to the company and that client, I was awarded a twenty-five percent raise and ultimately a promotion. Learning the new database language was not something that I was told to do nor was it something that I was paid to do or allocated time to learn during my normal work hours, but it was what I chose to do on my own time as part of my growth plan to move to the next level in my career. Adopting a growth plan and consistently following it throughout my professional life has not only led me to have a successful career with three major Silicon Valley companies but also to owning a thriving business for over twenty years. Personal growth is the bedrock to success. My mentor once shared with me, "don't wish things were easier but wish you grow better." The more you grow the easier things will become. If you grow, your problems around you will shrink. If you grow, the opportunities around you will grow.

Growth is not isolated to your job or career. Perhaps you want to grow your relationship with your spouse or significant other. There are people who have overcome the same challenges you have in your relationship, whether it is communication, intimacy, connection, joy, or any other area. As with any knowledge that you lack, the key is to identify a mentor, resource, or information to help you grow in that area. Trying to weather it alone will not support growth. My wife and I have now been married for 20 years. To strengthen our marriage, we have both focused on attending a marriage seminar annually and a commitment to consistent reading to deepen our understanding of what makes a successful marriage work. Whereas our marriage is not perfect, we are encouraged that every year our marriage has grown stronger and stronger with our commitment to make it grow.

The key to growth is going beyond learning information to taking action on the information you learn. Growth without action is just research. Oftentimes, self-development junkies confuse the process of learning with growth itself. But if one continues to research, study, and learn without ever taking action, they will soon become just a wise derelict. We all have the uncle or neighborhood guru that knows everything (or at least professes they do) and has all the answers and advice for you but they themselves haven't achieved anything. It is because they have never taken action. It is not enough to have a life spent learning without having a life spent taking action. For every area where growth is desired, you must identify milestones along the way. Just like mile markers along a driving route, they should be measurable. At each milestone, you must look back and reflect on the progress you have made and make adjustments if necessary for the road ahead. I laugh at myself because I almost never drive anywhere without using my navigation system. Every now and then, the road has a detour that forces me to take an unplanned turn. As soon as I do, the navigation system resets itself to map out the new route to my final destination. If you are constantly entering a new destination on your navigation system but never actually moving the car, you will never make any progress towards your goal. You must take action and make adjustments to the plan along the way. If recalculations and adjustments are necessary as we map our route to the mall, how much more important is it that we reflect and make adjustments as we map our way to our goals?

As unfruitful as it is to have a growth plan and never take action, it is equally as ineffective to always take action without having a growth plan. To do so would be like putting an octopus on roller skates. They may be moving every which way but not making any forward progress. As a man of action, I commonly mistook increase for growth. I thought that if I worked harder and harder, I would achieve success. But just because something is increasing doesn't mean it is growing. We all have heard of companies that sprout up and become the rave for a short period before the bubble bursts and the company no longer exists. Or, we know of the young athlete whose talent gets him into elite sports but character, maturity, and skills do not grow enough to keep him there. Worse than having not achieved success is to achieve it and lose it all because you haven't grown enough to sustain it. Lottery winners are more likely to file bankruptcy in three to five years than the average American. It is because their wealth increased overnight but they have not experienced the mindset growth needed to maintain the wealth so they quickly lose it. In every one of these examples, this was increase, not growth. No bodybuilder wins a competition because a muscle is swollen. The muscle must grow over a period of time with incremental increases in resistance until it builds in strength and size. Similarly, you cannot expect to grow overnight. It takes time, patience, and diligence. The process of growth is just as important as the result itself. One of my mentors taught me that the longest distance between two points is a shortcut. If you are looking for a quick fix, shortcut, or easy way to success you will find the fastest way to failure. Respect and embrace the process as much as you desire to embrace the result.

Now that we understand the real definition of growth, why it is critical to your success, and the results that it can produce, how do we begin to formulate a plan to execute on these principles? There are six core steps to formulating a growth plan for success. Whereas in the early years of my life, these steps were unconsciously taken, I was able to reflect back at how I had attained some early successes and later made them a conscious part of what has allowed me to obtain and sustain success in every area of my life.

Step 1: Identify the goal you want to achieve and write it down.

Step 2: Identify the skills that you must grow in order to achieve that goal.

Step 3: Commit to the daily activity of learning the skill through reading a book, listening to a CD or audio, studying a course, and/or conversing with a mentor.

Step 4: Identify key milestones along the journey to the goal so you can reflect back on your progress and adjust your plan accordingly.

Step 5: Get feedback on your progress from a mentor or expert that has achieved success in the area that you are focused on growing.

Step 6: On an annual basis, at the least, go back to Step 1 to ensure that the goal is still relevant to your life's purpose and change it or double down on your growth plan accordingly.

Now, to take immediate action on what you've learned, write down a goal for each of the four major areas of your life which include your personal relationships, career/vocation, health, and spirituality. Then, for each goal, follow the six-step process above to create your growth plan.

Just as optimum nutrition includes consumption of all major food groups, so must your plan include every step of what I outlined. My prayer for you, brother, is that you will take to heart all that I have shared, incorporate it into your life, and grow far beyond what you ever thought was possible.

Anwar Miller

Commit to Your Work

I retired from working for a major corporation after approximately thirty-nine years of service. During that time, I learned a variety of lessons that, even though it may have taken a few years to embrace, have served me well and led to a successful and rewarding career. My hope is that you will glean something from my experiences that will help you develop a commitment to your work that will lead you to the success you desire.

1. Develop and live by sound principles

   ○ All people deserve to be treated with respect and love unless they prove otherwise. It is a basic human need to be treated with love and respect. What you pour into your relationships directly impacts what you get out of them. Applying love and respect builds strong relationships that generate human currency that can be spent to enhance both your and your colleague's job performance. Plus, it's just the right thing to do!

   ○ Always do your job no matter what others are doing or how you may be treated. If you make your performance people dependent, your performance will go up and down. Consequently, you will have lapses in your job performance. Also, you will collect a paycheck for work you did not do, decrease your employee value, and make your job less interesting.

○ Learn to forgive. Nobody is perfect. If you wish to be forgiven for your mistakes then it is only right that you forgive others.

○ Respect the importance of all your jobs and assignments. Your historical performance becomes part of your legacy and can become a springboard for future opportunities. And remember, your performance reflects your skills and your character.

○ No matter what, always do the right thing. Do not be misguided by what others are doing. Personalize your decisions with moral and ethical filters. My Christian teachings have been my supreme guidance in applying this principle.

2. Follow the company's core values.

○ Core values reinforce community, provide direction, and target common accountabilities. (This should not be superseded by devaluing your character or jeopardizing your safety.)

3. Know and follow the formal rules

○ Unless you own the business, you must respect the right of the owners to run their business as they choose. Respectfully challenge the rules to make them better, but along the way, you must adhere to them.

○ Know the informal rules but be careful about which ones you follow. Though the informal rules might run the show, following some of them can destroy your character and ruin your integrity!

4. Diversify your learning experience and skills

○ Do not be too proud to accept a job or task outside of your normal assignment. Increased job knowledge and skills increase your value. Also, learn all you can about your company and job site. This will help you to better understand the overall goals, vision, and management endeavors.

5. Seek out good mentors

○ Consider different mentors for different things such as increasing your ability to get promoted, people interaction skills, and navigating through work-life issues. Also, mentor others. When you mentor others you help them and learn from them, thus creating a win-win situation for mentor and mentee!

6. Pursue excellence in everything you do

○ The pursuit of excellence will give you personal satisfaction, growth, and the respect of your colleagues. Great wonders can be accomplished when we persistently pursue excellence.

7. Practice continuous improvement

○ Always strive to get better. Improve what you do and how you do it. This begins by improving your thinking processes. Maybe you can't teach an old dog new tricks but we, as humans, can always learn more.

8. Be your sisters and brothers' keeper

   ○ Our long-term success depends on taking care of each other. As we supplement our strengths and weaknesses, we will synergistically create a stronger unit and a better work environment.

9. Be an avid reader

   ○ Reading increases your knowledge, vocabulary, and helps to make you an interesting person. The afore-mentioned is increased as you diversify your reading sources. I have also used some of my readings to serve as informal mentoring mechanisms. Thus, I have received guidance from many specialists in many fields of knowledge!

10. Be 100% responsible for what happens to you in life

    ○ Blaming others or situations for the bad in our life becomes a crutch, an excuse to not perform at our best. Get rid of the "I'm a victim" syndrome and replace it with "I am and will be victorious!" We cannot control everything that happens to us, but we can participate in making things better.

Life can be summed up as a series of choices we continually make as we navigate through and develop our life's story. May you continually make the right choice! Build your story on a great foundation and you will succeed in your work!

Isaac Brown Jr

Exemplify Work Ethic

As I reflect on my life and what has shaped me, two things are inextricably linked as a part of my early life through my high school years. Outside of attending school, the most vivid memories of how my time was spent are working on a farm and playing sports. I often think of how the virtues of work and the lessons learned from working hard on the farm and in sports have formed an unshakeable foundation for me. At this point in my life, I don't know how to extricate myself from work. As I support my sons as they grow and develop as teenagers, I impart some discussion about work daily. I constantly tell them that what they achieve in their school grading periods is a direct reflection of the work they put into the process. What they will reflect on years from now as young men is the sight of me going to work on a daily and consistent basis. Almost five decades of living continue to reinforce how valuable a healthy work ethic is.

"If you can walk, you can work."

"If you don't work, you don't eat."

"If you don't work, you will steal."

Those are probably the words I most remember from my grandparents, and I remind myself of these words often when I am
tired or lack motivation. I lived next door to my grandparents
and it was their second-generation farm that I grew up on. They
truly believed that you did not have to be mentally or physically
gifted to work and be successful. They were only able to attend
school through the eighth grade but I learned more from them
through their examples of hard work than anyone else. What
they taught me was that just showing up to work was half the
battle. With vegetables, cash crops, and animals to tend to, there
never seemed to be an off-season. They never had much but
they always woke up with a sense of purpose. Many times, during my personal and professional challenges, I think back on all
the things they worked to overcome. They did not simply pray
to overcome those obstacles but also had to do the work necessary. My uncle was the foreman on the farm and his example
of dedication to work is etched in my memory. There were so
many days when I watched him drag himself out of his house
and take gulps of cough medicine as he knew he had things to
accomplish. Watching him work when he was sick and vomit-
ing while working gave me no reason to ever expect pity. He
epitomized "if you can walk, you can work!" Working on the
farm was a world where excuses could not and would not be tol-
erated. With so many family members to support, "if you don't
work, you don't eat" was a very real outcome! While I did not
always enjoy the requirements of farm living, it was something I
could not escape and it clearly created a commitment within that
formed my appreciation for work.

"You may not be as talented but don't ever be outworked."

Those are words that my high school basketball coach ingrained in me as I was a very undersized high school center battling taller and bigger players every game. In all my memories of games I played, my teams were never admonished for losing if we worked hard and refused to quit. I was never the most talented player on my teams. From the time I learned to run as a child, my brother, cousins and I were playing any sport available to us. There were always various balls and related equipment at our disposal. It was always interesting that the only things we could leave the farm for were church, school, and sports. With that clearly in focus, we played every team sport that would have us. Sports became my passion and while I always knew I was not the most talented from a skill or athletic perspective, it was always apparent if I followed the coach's direction, took care of the details, and took the job most players did not want, I could always get playing time. I also learned that talent might make a player special but no talented player had the market cornered on effort. Effort could not be coached and would make up for talent deficits in most instances. This became my view of athletics and anything in life, particularly with professional vocations. My coach said that others may be more talented but don't let them outwork you and I've applied that in other areas of my life. While the common thought is that team sports unify, the unification really comes in the hours spent working and practicing with teammates. The overused adage of "blood, sweat, and tears" is real and that combination only comes from the committed work that is put in through sports. I have teammates to this day that I will always share a bond with because of what we went through in working as teammates. Some of our games are more memorable than any other achievements I have had in life. The work gave us purpose and unleashed passion. The work taught us how to sacrifice for a common goal. The work defined our dedication to each other. The work instilled in us the idea that we must forge on through adversity. The work would not allow us to quit and let each other down.

At some of my lowest points in life, work has served as the best distraction and motivator I have ever known. Throwing myself into work has been an incredible catharsis. When I have had many setbacks in my personal and professional life, I look to exhaust myself with work as it allows me to refocus and direct my energy. Through work, I have been able to care for so many people, both in my family and others I will never know. Work has taught me how to sacrifice for the good of others and make sure everyone can be successful. Outside of faith, work has been an equalizer that brings balance and certainty to my life. I recall always thinking that sports and farm life prepared me for a successful life but as I reflect deeper while writing this, sports and farm life were just the vehicles to impart work ethic to me. I did not realize at the time what grueling farm life and the sometimes painful preparation in sports were truly instilling in me. Although the farm and sports are in my rearview mirror, the need, desire, and purpose I find in work are unceasing.

Work disciplines us.
Work shapes us.
Work teaches us.

Work nurtures us.

Work feeds us.

Work cultivates us.

Work grows us.

Work creates us.

Chris Brooks

Be A Producer

As Black men, we are often challenged with the task of producing in many aspects of our lives. Despite the unique challenges we may face, there is little to no room for error or excuses. Whether it's dealing with mild to overt forms of paternalistic racism, bigotry, and discrimination or paying bills to meet responsibilities to our families. The livelihood and self-preservation of ourselves, our family, and our communities rely on our ability to produce things and create opportunities.

Being a productive person can lead to great enhancements that influence and uplift the people around you. By definition, a PRODUCER creates or supplies, goods, or services. We as humans can produce tangible things that can be seen with the naked eye, but we can also produce things that are less quantitative and hard to measure. We are always producing something, whether we know it or not. Some things we produce can be beneficial and other things can be detrimental to ourselves and our communities. In most cases, we are primarily responsible for what we produce! There will always be elements outside of yourself that can alter your production which makes it ever so important to become aware of the things required to be a good producer.

···◆◆◆◆···

A great example I often use is the story of two math teachers who taught twin brothers in separate schools. Both twins took the same subject in the same grade at the same time. Both twins had ambitions of becoming building engineers. For the sake of clarity, let us name the teachers Mr. High Expectations and Mr. Low Expectations. Mr. High Expectations provided a written syllabus with coursework, firm expectations, and goals. Mr. High Expectations also provided insight on how the twin would be able to apply what he learned to skilled trades and everyday activities. Mr. High Expectations gave verbal instruction and was interactive. He would challenge the twin by asking questions and exploring different learning methods to help him understand the assignment. He would provide homework, study guides, and sample quizzes to prepare the twin for tests. He also created incentives to motivate the twin to complete tasks and make learning fun and exciting. In addition, he provided encouragement and praise for the student's efforts and updated his parents on his progress.

However, the other twin taught by Mr. Low Expectations provided no written syllabus or minimal expectations of what to expect in class. He provided no goals for the coursework. Mr. Low Expectations provided minimal class instruction and often provided handouts with little guidance on how to solve problems. Mr. Low Expectations allowed the twin to watch videos and music during most of the class instruction. When the twin in Mr. Low Expectations' classroom struggled with assignments, he provided little feedback on how he could improve and gave no encouragement to do better. He also provided no communication to his parents regarding his poor performance. At the end of the course, the twin in Mr. Low Expectations' class ended up with a D+. While the twin in Mr. High Expectations' class received an A. The twin who received guidance from Mr. High Expectations went on to become an architect and now designs multimillion-dollar skyscrapers while the other twin ended up becoming a general laborer for the same company.

I am quite sure I do not have to tell you why Mr. Great Expectations produced a better student who had better outcomes! Both twins had the same potential but Mr. High Expectations simply put more time and effort into producing a better product. The more time and focused effort you give to producing the things you want, the better your outcomes. That rule is consistent with everything you do in life.

···◆◆◆···

The motivation that drives you to produce things to meet a need or a desire is often wrapped around your vision and purpose, your goals, and the standards you want to create for yourself, your family, and your community. Having a clear vision and purpose gives a better perspective on how you will see yourself in the future. Lastly, having good habits is the string that ties everything together.

Our vision and purpose are born from our creative imagination based on tangible outcomes that meet our desires and dreams. It can be sparked by our curiosity, our internal motivation to strive for greatness or it can even be sparked by dark and hopeless moments that fuel our passions to be more than the person we currently are.

Secondly, having a clear set of goals gives you a road map for making your vision and purpose a reality by creating tangible stages and action steps to help you reach certain outcomes. You must also identify and master your skills to help you produce the outcomes that you want. You must learn how to maximize your talent through obtaining more knowledge, practicing, and finding ways to constantly improve yourself. Lastly, create a standard that sets the bar for what you want or what you refuse to tolerate. As it relates to Black male children in this current era, there is often a void of guidance, role modeling, mentoring, discipline, and structure that often leads to a continuous cycle of low self-worth, criminality, hopelessness, complacency, and low productivity. We often suffer in silence because we do not set standards and expectations for ourselves or our community. When you do not set standards, you often fail to hold yourself accountable for your actions and your outcomes.

Additionally, after you have a clear understanding of what you want to produce through your goals, you must have good habits so you can execute to get the outcomes you want. Habits, in summary, are basic rituals and conditioned behaviors that you do consistently. Often poor habits lead to being a poor producer. Some important poor habits and rituals to avoid that lead to poor production include not having clear goals for your life, being around unproductive people who have no vision for themselves, procrastinating or waiting until the last minute to do things resulting in poor execution and performance, failing to plan, and self-sabotaging behaviors created by past hurts and past failures. Feeding into negative cultural stereotypes that promote ignorant and risky behavior and not taking care of your health and your body leading to less mental clarity and less energy to produce results at high levels are also important habits to avoid.

In summary, I challenge each of you to be a producer. You can apply this knowledge to yourself or to help others. As Black men, it is important to understand that those generations before you, in some way, shape or form, have sown into your life to make better outcomes for yourself and your community. Marcus Garvey produced pride and dignity in the hearts and souls of the Black race that ignited the will of self-empowerment. Martin Luther King, Jr. produced change by challenging a nation to live up to its creed of liberty and justice for all. Thurgood Marshall produced a legal movement that led to our ability to receive equal access to education that opened doors for Black men and women to become scientists, doctors, and astronauts. The Greensboro Four and students at North Carolina A&T State University produced inspiration for change with the sit-in movement that created nationwide protests that eventually gave Blacks the right to eat at restaurants without fear of harm or rejection. Colin Kaepernick produced a movement that inspired Black athletes and citizens of all colors and nationalities to advocate against police brutality and an unfair criminal justice system that marginalizes poor people and people of color.

Everyone was put on this Earth to produce something. Your vision and purpose may be similar to or different from others, but what you produce is no more or less important in your quest to be productive for the good of mankind. You do not have to win a Nobel Peace Prize or give away a million dollars to make effective change. Find a need in your community, identify skill sets, gifts or resources you may have, and apply yourself to meet those needs. It could be as simple as volunteering at a youth detention center or mentoring a young child in the community. It could be as easy as providing scholarship money to a needy child at a local school or paying into a school lunch account to make sure a child does not have to go hungry during lunchtime. It could be as simple as attending your local city council meeting to ensure your community receives the help and support it needs to thrive.

We can no longer wait for our government, a billionaire, or Jesus to save us. We have the skills, resources, and gifts to be a producer of great things but what you produce will be up to you! It is up to you to produce the change you want to see within your community and within yourself.

Kevin Walker

Overcome Obstacles

This letter was first written as my testimony. Only through the experiences I have embraced, which have equated to successes and failures, have I become qualified enough to broach the subject presented here. Before we embrace the strategies of overcoming obstacles, it is critical that we first understand that the concepts involved are not derived from novel ideas. The ability to overcome obstacles is rooted in the depths of the Black experience. Many of our cultural abilities, especially our unparalleled social and economic resourcefulness, have been well-documented and, when further examined, often appear superhuman. The degree of social and economic resourcefulness developed within the Black community is inarguably a powerful effect of the unique situations we have been forced into. Historically, we have been disenfranchised and forced to negotiate a shaky ladder to upward mobility. Yet, we are continuously adapting and progressing toward social and economic prosperity. Although we have been left bereft of privilege, our innovative and collective works have resulted in incalculable feats. Although we have too often been depicted as large shadows looming over the grandeur of this nation, let us not forget that it was our use of resourcefulness, amongst other tools, that made this nation. It is these same tools of resourcefulness, audacity, and faith that we will now use to make a man.

Brothers, as we work together to make a man, let us assure he is one imbued with the spirit of an overcomer. The word *overcomer*, which derives from the Greek word *Nike*, means "to carry off the victory" and implies a battle.[12] As an infantry leader in the U.S Army and scholar of military history, I can attest to the following: battles are not won by the weak or timid; and, psychologically, not all men are equipped for battle. Some quiver and quail when engaged in conflict. I cannot attest to your reaction when faced with conflict, whether you are more attuned to the fight or flight response, but I can equip you for your battles in the moments you remain steadfast. I have spent the last decade invested in the development of warfighters. I have spent a long period of time studying the greatest military leaders. What I have learned is that every historically great military leader possessed an audacious character. As with resourcefulness, possessing an audacious character is critical to overcoming obstacles because it means that the individual is unrestrained in a conventional manner. Brothers, we were never meant to be sheepish. We were made to be lionhearted. In fact, it is our bold spirit that contributes to the white fear of Black men in America. Despite the adversity our community has faced, our heads have remained unbowed. Despite our unique conditions, we have perpetually refused to adopt a defeated mindset. We never minimized ourselves for white magnitude. We have never apologized for our existence. We have never stayed put and stayed quiet. And, when we were told to "shut up and dribble," we used our athletic platforms as a tool for political awareness versus taking our ball and going home. Brothers, we are powerful beyond measure. In fact, the only person that could possibly get in our way and lead to our defeat is ourselves. Typically, it is the uncertainties in our individual talents that limit our progress. In reading this, I challenge you to stop impeding your own progress. Adopt a spirit of audacity in your works, faith, relationships, and obstacles. Be prideful, yet remain humble, in the work that you produce. Become more connected with your faith and strengthen your relationship with God. Be intentional, not dismayed, in dealing with your obstacles by consistently displaying intrepidity, resilience, and faith.

Faith has many meanings in society, sacred texts, and personal understandings. Hebrews 11:1 (KJV) reads, "Now faith is the substance of things hoped for, the evidence of things not seen." Faith is an essential element to the chemistry of life and with an absence of faith, there is a presence of despair. Brothers, no man is made without faith, but every man will go through periods where it is tested. Therefore, as we use tools of success to make a man, it is important to ensure that faith is properly tightened in his being. The faith we weld into our sons will be periodically tested by life and God. As fire forges steel, so will our experiences forge our character. Our faith must remain resolute, less we bend to adversity. 1 Peter 1:7 (NKJV) states, "that the genuineness of your faith, *being* much more precious than gold that perishes, though it is tested by fire, may be found to praise, honor, and glory at the revelation of Jesus Christ." Faith has four major functions in our lives: Faith empowers us during moments of crisis by continuing to provide us with strength (Isaiah 40:31 KJV). Faith gives us stability by connecting us to communities of people with similar beliefs from which we can receive support (Romans 15:2 NKJV). Faith grants us the ability to encourage others through our displays of righteousness (Titus 1:7 NLT). Lastly, faith gives us hope through the promise of victory. "For everyone who has been born of God overcomes the world. And this is the victory that has overcome the world—our faith" (1 John 5:4 ESV). Brothers, of the tools I have mentioned in this letter, faith is arguably the most essential tool in overcoming obstacles. It is inarguably the one that will be the most tested. Maintaining a resourceful and audacious character will help to pass the test.

Brothers, I pray that you adopt the tools left with you in this letter and use them in your personal endeavors as our community always has. Our innate sense of resourcefulness, boldness in action, and faith have historically served as a compass towards prosperity in our most trying times. I will now leave you with one last concept designed to help you navigate through your obstacles. This concept is understanding that the process we use to negotiate difficult terrain is as important as the outcome. The lessons learned between the inception and conclusion of a problem become our experience or our testimony. It is our testimony that will encourage others to resolve their problems. In the beginning, I stated that this letter was first written as my testimony. It is through my testimony that I have become equipped with the tools necessary in helping you understand yours. Consider this, in many of the classes we had in school we were told to show our work as we find the solution to our problems. We were not told this for our own benefit. We were told this so that whoever was assessing our work could better understand how we resolved the problem. Our testimonies have equivalent importance. When others are made aware of how we resolve our problems, they become aware of two other important things as well: effective methods in resolving their own conflict and that prosperity is possible. Thus, I implore you to appreciate your process and remember that your testimony will one day serve as an inspiration to others.

Brothers, I impart these words to you with the utmost love and respect. I pray they fulfill their purposes in providing mental and spiritual nourishment. May this letter serve you in your most demanding moments and may the concepts enclosed within help you to become the best version of yourself.

Channon L. Rothmiller

Demonstrate Grit

I want you to learn about a topic that is so crucial to your growth as a man. I feel if I don't tell you, I would be doing you a grave injustice. As you move through this world, you will be told many things about what you need to do to have a successful journey in life. You will hear suggestions like work hard, do the right thing, treat people as you want to be treated, your friends are your future, don't lie, cheat or steal, and so on. All of this will be true and great advice. However, I want to tell you two related stories that will teach you about what I believe is one of the most important traits a young man must have in order to end up being the man he wants to be.

The first story is about a young male teacher who has a student who, after doing so well at the beginning of the school year, had been missing school and falling asleep in class. The young man seemed to be very distant and unresponsive to the teacher's requests to pay attention and do his work. After a few weeks of this, the teacher decided to call home to address the issue with the parents. During the conversation with the parents, the teacher realizes that both parents seem to be high on drugs but, obviously, he couldn't prove that to be true. The teacher called his student to the hallway the next day to ask about his home life as sensitively as he could under the circumstances. The student eventually admitted that his parents are struggling with addiction issues. The teacher then asks the student if he is taking care of his younger sister and the parents? The student said yes. It is then that the teacher told him that life at this point is going to be tough for him, but that he didn't want the student to give up. "I want you to get through this challenging time and learn from it as much as possible. It will be difficult, as life can be at times, but it will make you grow as a person." The teacher offered to give assistance when needed. That student ended up graduating that same school year. He even maintained good standing at his after-school job as he supported his family.

The second story is about a college football team that just made the transition from a small two-year junior college to a four-year division three college. During such a transition, teams usually play competition that is similar to themselves. The current coach did not want to do that. He wanted to play against the best colleges immediately. He believed that to be the best, you had to beat the best. That would seem to be a very challenging task for this team made up of mostly freshmen, some of whom hadn't played high school football. They would be playing against mostly upperclassmen. The team lost every game leading up to the final game of the season. Now they were going to play the number one rated division three team in the country. At this point, only 27 players remained on the team that started out with 85 players. The college president called a meeting to ask the remaining players if they wanted to forfeit the game so as to not get injured or embarrassed. During the meeting, some players were debating about whether to play. One player stood up and yelled, "This is football! We are going to go down there and play them the same way we've played against all the other teams on our schedule. We cannot run from this challenge or our program is doomed to fail." The team decided to play the game. They would lose the game by the score of 75-6. Even though they suffered such an embarrassing defeat, they learned a valuable lesson by not quitting. They learned about grit!

Grit is why I am writing you this letter. Passion plus perseverance equals grit. Although all the tools of success I mentioned previously are very important, having grit is a characteristic that is crucial to having the success you seek and to becoming the man you want to be. During life, you will have adversity or challenges that will shock your world. Difficult situations will arise. You will treat people with respect only to have them turn around and disrespect you. You will study for a test and fail the test. If you play sports, you will train and prepare for the game and still lose. You may suffer a bodily injury or physical ailment. You may have an unexpected death of someone you treasure and love. People you trusted may let you down. A relationship will end. Life challenges will sometimes seem unbearable. It is then that you must learn to grow through the experiences you go through. The way to prepare for these challenges is like anything else, you must practice. By practice, I mean to accept the challenges of everything you enjoy doing or want to do. Accept your failures as a lesson learned. It has been shown that many people are very successful for the majority of their life but fall apart at the first failure that occurs.

Those people, most of the time, did not take enough chances to experience small defeats that would prepare them for a major defeat. Then they find it difficult to handle challenges. I want you to always do what you love to do, therefore making it worth accepting the challenges that come with it. It has also been proven that people who do what they love to do are the happiest and healthiest. Find what you love to do, and you will do it with great success. Challenges from those endeavors will be lessons taught to overcome greater challenges. Loving what you do brings out the passion for what you do. When you have that passion, it becomes easier to exhibit perseverance for any of life's unexpected challenging events.

Another part of preparing for life's challenges is being where you are supposed to be. No matter what the situation is, it is important that you show up. People will believe in someone who is timely and considerate of another's time. I remember one of my mentors emphasizing the phrase "be here now." The emphasis was on being in every moment that is in front of you. You can't accomplish your goals when you are not where you are supposed to be whether it is being there physically or mentally.

This brings me back to the stories I've shared. The student previously mentioned is doing great in his chosen career. His mother and father received help after he told the right people about their issues. His sister is going into high school. The college football team I mentioned went on to lose 27 straight games before they won for the first time in that division. Again, those players showed another aspect of having grit.

They maintained a goal and struggled to accomplish it over a long period of time. It wasn't just showing up for that one game. It was the team's grit that got them through years of disappointments to arrive at their goal of being a top-rated organization. The interesting part about that story is the young man who stood up and yelled about how they must play the game and accept the challenge. That young man has a story of grit. He would eventually lose his brother three months later to suicide. But he still continued on and graduated from college. He would be the only player from the original 85 team members that would not quit the team or transfer because the team was doing so badly. He would be the backbone of their future success. Because that team showed up and played, they left a legacy of grit. That college football team twenty-five years later, is now one of the top four division three teams in the country every year. Also, that player who stood up and wanted to play would go on to be that teacher who encouraged his student to show his grit and persevere through the challenges his family was facing. He was a teacher who never missed a day of work in his entire career. Because he believed showing up for his students was the first step in developing grit in them. I hope someday you will also teach these lessons to other young men. Like I've been telling you throughout this letter, grit will be the most crucial characteristic you need to develop to accomplish all that you set out to do. I trust that you will do exactly that.

Calvin Griffin

Replenish Yourself

Learning how to replenish yourself is one of the biggest aspects of becoming a man. When you do so, it refreshes you and helps to build you or help you to grow as you go through life. Allow me to share how the commitment to replenishing myself has made me a better man as an individual and how it can make better men in society.

From a young age, I have always strived to be better than I was the day before. The only way that I can see real growth is when I reflect on where I am and make the necessary changes to get where I want to go. I can't blame anyone else; I can't make excuses. I have to sit down and think, "What can YOU do to be great. What can YOU do to make a greater impact." My senior year of high school was one of the major experiences that shaped me into who and how I am today. As an aspiring college athlete, I was able to have a couple of "looks" to play college football at the next level by the end of my junior year.

All summer, I was putting in the work, gaining interest from different schools, training, and preparing myself for that next level. Prior to the first game of the season, my coach had full faith in me to start and contribute to making a deep run in the playoffs. After the season opener, however, I realized that this season was going to be about much more than football. As the season progressed, I contributed to the team a lot but not like I should have. Coaches played their favorites, and it really took a toll on me mentally. I would think to myself, "I put in the work. I've proven myself as a leader. I'm making plays. I do everything I need to do, so why isn't it enough?" At this point in the season, I had a heart-to-heart with God and talked to my parents as well. This was when I really started to replenish myself as a man. I ultimately gained the mindset where I refused to stress over things that I have no control over. All I could do, as it pertained to football was be the best athlete on that field at every opportunity I was given.

Replenishing myself gave me a mental edge; an unbreakable mindset. Even when things were not going well, I still maintained confidence, the college offers still came, and I was having a great experience during my senior and final year of high school football. So, when the playoffs came around, we had a long way to go if we wanted to win districts. The week leading up to the game in practice really tested me mentally. Even while I dominated in practice, being nearly flawless and making plays in games, the coaches decided to limit my role in the offense even when it wasn't called for.

However, this made me stronger. I replenished myself once more and used this as fuel and focused on making a play for my team whenever I touched the ball. And that is exactly what I did. In the final high school game of my career, I finished with 80 yards on 10 yards per carry, scoring the only touchdown for my team. I was proud of myself and content with the outcome because I could say that I left everything on the field and gave it my all. To sum this up, my senior year of high school football had many ups and downs. But in replenishing myself mentally, it helped me to weather the storm. I still had the opportunity to play Division 2 or Division 3 football, which was my goal. But that was just the surface. Digging deeper, my experiences during my senior year have stuck with me to this day. I've learned to evaluate situations from a personal aspect–what can you do, what is your role, how can you change. That is what I want you to take from this. When you focus on replenishing yourself, it helps you to elevate your manhood and be a better version of yourself. This is what Black men need to work on. We need to take accountability for not just our actions, but every area of our lives.

When you replenish yourself–build yourself up, reset your mindset, pour into you–you can get to the next level in your life, business or career more easily. Now, as a Black man, I can say that mental health is essential and the lack of attention to it has led to a lot of my brothers' downfall. It's okay to not be okay. It's okay to talk to someone about your problems and to seek help with issues in your life instead of trying to mask them because of pride or masculinity. Yes, you should replenish yourself but when you are empty and do not have the ability to do so, you must seek the help of others, even experts, to help replenish you. Put as much focus on your mental, emotional, and spiritual development as you do your physical and financial development. You deserve to be whole, healed, and well–and our communities need you to be–but that does not come without you taking time to focus on yourself.

Jordan Spencer

Manage Your Health

Brothers, there is nothing more important than your health. My guess is that you've probably heard this before. I'd also guess that unless you've been touched by an illness that brought you down for a significant amount of time, you probably take your health for granted. Don't worry. You're not alone. Most people do, but Black men, in particular, are highly likely to see themselves as invincible. The thing is, statistically speaking, this sense of invincibility is unwarranted and a reality check is in order. None of us is Superman®. Sooner or later disease comes for all of us. It's just a fact of life. You either have been sick or you will be sick. When disease strikes it either makes life difficult or it changes your life forever and threatens to kill you.

Cancer is one of the things that threatens to kill you. The death rate for all African American men who died of Cancer is 21%.[13] That's almost one in every four deaths. Heart disease, diabetes, high blood pressure, stroke, all of these ailments loom large over the African American community. And what about 'Rona? It is killing Black men at dramatically higher rates than white men.

123

So, with all of these viable threats to your life what are you prepared to do? Do you have a plan? How will you protect yourself? How will you protect your way of life? If you were a professional athlete, your health would be a priority and you would pay close attention to your physical fitness. You would build your body and fuel it with nutrition to arm yourself with the energy and strength required to overpower your competition. Gentlemen, I respectfully believe that we have a higher calling than football players. We are fathers, husbands, and sons. Our children, our wives, and our parents need our protection. You have gifts that your family and even the larger community stand in vital need of; however, in order to pour into the lives of anyone else you have to be on your feet. You have a responsibility to manage your health. What's the best way to get back in the game when you're sidelined by sickness? Better yet, what's the best way to avoid getting sick altogether?

In the beginning, God created a perfect world for man and called it the Garden of Eden. It was a utopia full of lush vegetation, colorful plant life, and aromatic herbs. Four rivers flowed through the garden watering everything in sight and the fresh garden air was filled with the sound of sparkling waterfalls crashing on the rocks below. Then God created Adam and Eve and put them in the garden. They had everything they needed. They didn't have to work. They didn't have to plant anything themselves. God supplied all of their needs and told them to eat everything in the garden except for the fruit of one tree. You probably know the story. Adam and Eve had a perfect situation but they messed it up by eating from the one tree God told them not to eat from and the rest is history.

But here's the point: Before God created a man and a woman he created a garden to put them in. Not a farm, a garden, and Adam and Eve only ate what was in the garden. We were meant to eat a plant-based diet. Actually, we were designed to eat a plant-only diet.

Today's Standard American Diet is literally *sad*. Beef and chicken make up a large part of this diet, yet they are full of carcinogens and other disease-promoting compounds. Hot dogs are considered to be *the* all-American food, but the World Health Organization has listed hot dogs as a Group 1 Carcinogen. Cigarettes are also listed as a Group 1 Carcinogen. This means that hot dogs should come packaged with a warning from the surgeon general because they are just as likely to cause cancer as cigarettes. But it's not just hot dogs. All processed meats carry this same dangerous distinction. This means the bacon and sausage you eat for breakfast can cause cancer. Lunch meats like bologna, ham, and turkey can cause cancer. The sausage and pepperoni on that pizza can cause cancer. All of these processed meats are huge sellers. Many of us eat them every day. We feed them to our children. At a very young age, we begin to eat dangerous carcinogens with our food. How much damage will these processed meats do to the developing body of a child?

Dairy products like cheese, butter, eggs, and milk all create mucus and mucus promotes disease. If you are still drinking cow's milk you should consider switching to an alternative like almond milk immediately. I know, you thought milk from a cow "does a body good," well it does, but only if the body belongs to a baby cow. Cow's milk is designed to facilitate the growth of a calf into a 1,100 lb adult cow or a 2,200 lb bull. For people, however, a mother's breast milk is the single best thing for a baby.

Fact #1: Humans are the only creatures on earth that regularly drink the milk of another creature. It's actually pretty gross when you think about it.

Fact #2: Humans are the only creatures on earth that drink milk beyond infancy. Once animals grow teeth they leave milk behind, but not us.

Fact #3: 65% of everyone in the world is thought to be lactose intolerant; meaning they are either unable to digest or experience difficulty digesting the sugar in cow milk. That percentage is even higher for people of African descent. If even after all of that processing, pasteurizing, and homogenizing only 4 out of 10 people can safely drink milk, maybe that's an indication that we shouldn't drink it.

So what happens to someone who stops eating beef, poultry, processed meats, eggs, cheese, and butter, and replaces cow's milk with almond milk, and converts to a plant-based diet?

In June of 2020, my 65-year-old cousin was diagnosed with prostate cancer. He could not walk because his cancer had progressed to stage 4 and had gotten into his bones, particularly his knees. Once cancer enters stage 4 it is considered terminal; so with the belief that there was nothing more they could do the medical professionals at the hospital sent him home, ostensibly to die. I moved in with Mike to care for him and immediately switched him to a plant-based diet. I did all of his shopping and cooked all of his meals. I eliminated all dairy products and replaced whatever I could with plant-based alternatives. No more bacon and eggs. No more traditional cheeseburgers or sodas. I went heavy on the fruits and made him a smoothie every morning with lemon, banana, strawberries, blueberries, blackberries, raspberries and, since it was summer, I included cherries, which have strong cancer-fighting properties. Mike enjoyed his food, especially the chipotle black bean burgers with dairy-free cheese that I made him for lunch. It wasn't long before Mike started making progress. He regained movement in his knees and started walking around his room. In August, he started walking up and down the stairs, then one day he went outside and took a walk around the block. In September, Mike went to see his doctor and was told that the markers they counted to determine that he had cancer were down to levels "less than zero," but they stopped short of declaring him cancer-free. Instead, his doctor said that if Mike had shown up in June with levels that low he would not have started the cancer protocols.

The human body is amazing. It's designed to heal itself and run for over 100 years, but like a fine automobile, it requires the proper fuel, and anything of lower quality compromises performance. Some of the things we are eating are killing us because we're simply not designed to consume them. Fast food, junk food, pizzas, and animal products all compromise the performance of the human body and there are billion-dollar industries that depend on your ignorance of this simple truth to survive. These industries have powerful lobbies and spend millions of dollars to ensure their survival, not yours. Their mission is to get you to add to their bottom line. History teaches us that Black men cannot afford to leave their well being in the hands of others. You are responsible for your health. An educated Black man is the most feared creature on earth, so educate yourself. There are many books, documentaries, and resources that endorse the benefits of a plant-based diet. We can only do better once we know better and now you know that a few simple changes will make a world of difference. A king gives life to his family so spread the word. There are countless benefits to eating a plant-based diet. Fighting cancer is but one of them.

Remember Adam in the Garden of Eden? According to Genesis 5, he lived to be 930 years old, and he never took a single pill for high blood pressure or cholesterol (although Adam lived for 930 years, your results may vary). Whether you want to restore a loved one to good health or protect your own, eat plants.

James Pair

UNITE COMMUNITY

"We choose hope over fear. We see the future not as something out of our control, but as something we can shape for the better through concerted and collective effort."

Former U.S. President,
Barack Obama

Understand Your Role

Brother, reflect on the communities that you are a part of, the values that unite their members, and most importantly, the role that you play. Everyone who is a part of a community plays a role in upholding its values and the values instilled by the community help define their role. In my personal opinion, each member of a community should ultimately seek to keep it united and they do so by sharing common values. Whether you're a part of a sports team, workplace, religious practice, political party, or social activist group, every member is brought together under common goals, values, and experiences.

Like most, the first community I belonged to was my family. In my early membership, I learned the values that united us as a family: loving others, respecting others and oneself, educating others and oneself, being of service, having accountability, and humility. Over time, my role within my familial community has evolved from a son, brother, cousin and nephew to also now a husband, uncle, and hopefully a father when the time comes! However, even though my role has evolved over time, I recognize that my ultimate role is to uphold the values that were instilled in me during my early membership and to hold other members (new or old, old or young) to those values as well. As you can see, you can have multiple roles in a community but one question remains constant across those roles: How are you upholding the core values of the community so that it remains united as it grows? After much reflection, I've come to understand that my familial community set the foundation for how I would define my own role within other communities that I would eventually join.

Learning to respectfully challenge the status quo is another value that was instilled in me early on. I have learned that this is a practice that directly applies to holding a community accountable to its values and purpose. How so? I strongly believe that my communities are an extension of who I am which is defined by the foundational values that I hold myself to on a daily basis.

I've been involved in many different communities throughout my life aside from my own family. Until high school, I was an active member of the Catholic community. I've also been a part of high school and collegiate football and track teams. In college, I joined campus support and productivity groups like the Students Organized for Black and Hispanic Unity (SOBHU) and Physics-major study groups. I also have been a part of a variety of Employee Resource Groups (ERGs) at different employers. I've had to challenge these communities in different ways so that 1) I can align my values, 2) Better understand my role and how that contributes to the overall success of uniting the community, and 3) Ultimately determine whether I should remain a part of the community going forward.

I learned early on what it felt like to be a part of a divisive community. I was part of a middle school community that struggled with bullying culture. In the instances where I had to face bullies for harassing me or other students, I had to put my values of love, respect, and self-respect at the forefront to combat these challenges. While submerged in this environment, I asked myself, "Do I belong here? Does this community support me?" Thankfully, I could rely on other community members–friends and teachers–to stay true to the community values. They taught me that it was important to define my role no matter the environment.

In a specific case, I learned that gaining clarity of the role I wish to play can create conflict with the community. In this case, it resulted in my leaving a community to which I belonged for many years. I was raised in a religious household and attended Sunday school most of my childhood. As I grew older, I came to realize that some of my values conflicted with the teachings and traditions of the church. I made the difficult decision that while I would respect the values I've been taught, I will redefine my relationship with my spirituality.

Later in my life, I attended a Predominantly White Institution (PWI) and it was a culture shock for me. Not just because of the racial disparity but also the socio-economic differences. So many different students from different parts of the world brought together for the goals of education and educating oneself. What about other core values? The values of respect, treating others equally, judging others on the content of their character and not the color of their skin? Recognizing that the college administration needed to do a better job at unifying the community allowed me to navigate sub-communities where I was able to strategize with others with those shared values to unite the greater college community. SOBHU played a major role in my life in better understanding my role in this new environment as a Black man. We supported each other at campus events, hosted a die-in, marched across the campus to protest against police brutality, and dove into Black culture through shared courses and community discussion forums. These experiences taught me the value and power of collective action. The SOBHU community is an extension of who I am and allowed me to express a better sense of self.

As I transitioned into the "real-world," my first job out of college was a sales entry role at a small tech company. After being almost four months into my role, a co-worker shouted a racial slur in a meeting room after his frustration for not finding his presentation slides. I won't get into the details but let's just say that he never came back to his desk that day. The company leadership took this matter very seriously and immediately let him go. The company leadership stepped into their role and upheld their values of respect and respecting others and determined that he could no longer be a member of the community.

After the situation, I asked myself a bunch of questions: How did the company allow someone like that to be a part of the community? Are there others who are as ignorant as him who may hold those same values? What about the next Black man or woman that walks through the door? How can we protect their psychological safety? Even though I was in an entry role by definition, intersections between my familial and SOBHU communities awoke my ultimate role. This was more than just a job for me. This is about my brother, my cousin, my nephew, my future son, or any person of color. When they walk through that company door or any door, I never want them to feel the way I did in that meeting room that day.

This event led me and a few other talented co-workers to collaborate with the leaders of the company to create the first-ever Employee Resource Group for the Black employee communities. This group today serves as a sub-community support system that plays a crucial role in holding the broader company community accountable to the values of respect, treating others equally, and judging others on the content of their character, the quality of their work, and not by the color of their skin. This is a role that I will continue to play for the rest of my career.

I will never forget how isolating and frustrating it felt to be a part of a divisive environment. The members of that environment might change, but still, it remains important to use my voice and hold the members of that community accountable. I truly believe that unity and inclusion are sacred because we each have something unique to contribute. However, unity is fragile and it requires each member to do their part.

I was walking to the store one day in DC and a brother in his car rolled down his window as I walked by. He shouted the words, "I love you, Black man." This caught me off guard in a good way because it was a rare interaction for me in the world of today and I responded, "Love you too, King." This brief moment, with a total stranger, reminded me of the value of love as the ultimate form of unification within any community. Whatever community you choose to belong to throughout your life, always remember that your foundational values will allow you to learn more about who you are and your role as you navigate and participate in the worldly community.

So I leave you with these questions for self-reflection: What unites you to the communities to which you belong? What values are these communities instilling in you and how are you reciprocating? How are you elevating others within the community that you share? How will you work to ensure that this community ultimately remains united?

Nick Joseph

Embrace Family

Embrace is to hug, cherish and love, to accept or support willingly and enthusiastically. Family, however, can mean a lot of different things to different people. What does that mean to you?

To me, family is more than just someone who has your last name or someone who is in your bloodline. Family is someone who will accept and support you willingly. Someone who doesn't see your failures, only your enthusiasm to pursue your dreams and goals, and if it doesn't work the first time they encourage you to get up and keep going. Family is someone that, no matter what, will be there. Family is someone that will love you enough to tell you when you are not doing what you are supposed to in order to achieve and become a better you. Family is someone who is your biggest supporter through the good times as well as the bad.

Now that I have said that, some of you might be thinking, "That's great but I don't have that in my life. I don't have a family like that." If you don't have a friend or a family member like that, due to whatever circumstance, then it's up to you to be that person for someone else. It has to start somewhere.

As I sat gathering my thoughts on how I was going to express them on paper, I went through many different scenarios in my life. I began to reflect on the good times and the celebrations of achievements that I have experienced. I also reminisced about some of the not so memorable moments in my life. While doing so, the one constant through all of it was family. Now, I'm not saying that family is the answer to everything but in my opinion, it is the answer to most things. See, there is no greater feeling than when you have family and the love that goes along with it.

With a strong family support system, there is nothing that you can't achieve. We, as young and mature Black men, should make family a priority. For so long, we have been stereotyped as not caring about our family. It's time that we change that negative image. As Black men, we may not have had an example of a strong family bond but that doesn't mean that it can't be achieved. You be that change; you be the difference in your family tree moving forward. When the family bond is strong nothing can break it or come between it.

I want to share a little part of my story with you. I was raised by my grandmother in Virginia, my father's mother. Growing up in what I called the country, we didn't have much but we always had each other. There were no silver spoons in anyone's mouth and sometimes we had to scrape by to make ends meet... and we did. Through the good times and the not so pleasant times, my grandmother always talked about family and what it meant. Being close, treating each other with respect, and having patience was a staple in her home. If you had a disagreement about something, she would let you express yourself and give you a few minutes to be upset or angry about it, and then she would say, "No matter what happens, we are family."

As I mentioned earlier, my grandmother raised me, as well as my sisters. Our parents were present and engaged but they lived up north. They did not want us growing up there and being latch key kids because they were both working.

My parents' decision was probably the best thing that ever happened to us. Instead of coming home and being there alone, we were constantly surrounded by family. My dad had six brothers and a sister. I was the oldest grandchild and also the only grandson, so my uncles raised me like I was the youngest brother to them. Now, sometimes that was a good thing, and other times, not so much. If I got into any type of trouble, I not only had to answer to my dad but all six of his brothers. That was something that I did not want to do. They would always say to me "we are family and everything you do reflects on all of us." I took that to heart and never wanted to be the person to cast a shadow on our family.

I saw the examples they set in keeping family first. I saw what it meant to grow up and treat others with respect. And, most of all, I saw what it meant to be a man, a Black man.

I watched their work habits and the pride they took in whatever task they were doing. I watched how they treated their wives and their children. I watched them and I saw how they treated each other. No matter what went on, family always came first.

Even now that I am an adult and have adult children of my own, I often look back at the example of family that was taught to me. My dad and his brothers are still setting the example of what family means. Every year they take a guys' trip somewhere just to spend some quality time together as brothers and I get to tag along to witness their example. Family is everything and we as Black men have to set that example for others.

In closing, I say to my fellow brothers, embrace your family, love one another, and be the example of what family really means.

Gary Walker

Elevate the Black Woman

First and foremost, allow me to congratulate you on making it this far. Considering a lot of people aren't able to reach such a feat, it's only right to give you your flowers. You're becoming a man. You are going to go out into the world and become a force and positive beacon of light. Don't be afraid to let your light shine.

Being a man is hard; especially being a Black man. It is up to us to captivate, educate, protect, and inspire our families, our communities, and most importantly, our children. Being a man comes with a laundry list of responsibilities–one of them being the inspiration for this writing, which is elevating the Black woman. The task of elevating the Black woman is no easy feat, but it is a necessary one. As you step into manhood, you will discover just how much this one task can make a difference.

History Lesson: the Black woman is one of the most underappreciated people on the planet earth–many will tell you differently. In my experience, she has worn and continues to wear a plethora of hats and adding new ones daily. She is our mother, our aunt, sister, cousin, girlfriend, friend, partner, teacher, nurse, nurturer–you name it, she has a hat for it. The true strength of the Black woman has been realized for a long time, hence why she has been treated and used in such a manner that seeks to strip her of her natural-born superpowers (they are failing, but they keep trying). She has been taking on and sharing in the hurt and the pain of the Black man since the dawn of time. We go to her for love, care, affection, sex, guidance, support, and so much more.

I'm sure you're wondering, "Why do we need to do this? How do we go about elevating the Black woman?" The answer is simple, yet complex. We need the Black woman. We came from a woman, got our name from a woman–sound familiar? That's because these are lyrics from Tupac Shakur's song entitled, "Keep Ya Head Up" from his February 1993 album release, Strictly for My N.I.G.G.A.Z.[14] The Black woman is an essential partner of the Black man. She is everything and more. As a whole, she is often criticized on a global scale for things she has and hasn't done. The last thing she needs is her male counterpart joining in on the bashing. As a man, one of your many jobs is to protect your wife and family. So, how do we elevate the Black woman? Rules of thumb to follow in elevating the Black woman are: make her feel secure, celebrate her, and most importantly, love her how she needs to be loved.

···◆◆◆···

All women, regardless of race or ethnicity, need to feel a sense of security. It bears repeating that Black women, especially in our current social climate, are one of the most underappreciated and disrespected persons in the world. The Black woman is at her best when she feels a level of security and protection. It is this level of protection that allows her to have a calm sense and build a sense of trust. Trust is very important to a Black woman. Building trust allows her to truly open up to you in ways you may have never imagined; something she can only do if she feels secure.

The first initial thought for yourself and many others entering manhood is, "I can keep her safe and provide that security." This is true. Physically, the woman absolutely wants her man to make her feel secure. However, providing security to a Black woman is much deeper than being able to physically keep her safe. It is also making her feel secure financially and mentally. Financially, a man has been placed at the head of the household as provider. Being secure in finances helps to keep your woman at ease. That is not to say there shouldn't be boundaries and budgets in place, but there are some must-haves that will provide this level of security that she is looking for. For example, the ability to work a functioning budget, manage or help manage the household bills and investing and putting money towards future goals is an important way to bring security to your woman. Having and holding steady employment or running a thriving company are also ways of providing financial security. She wants to know that her man has everything handled–and you will.

As important as it is to maintain financial security, it is equally important to provide a level of security for her mental stability. When one is attacked as often as the Black woman for any and every choice that she makes, the man is one of the first places she will turn in order to combat any mental anguish that has been brought on by the day. This may be the most important form of security a man needs to provide to the Black woman. In order to protect and provide the needed security for her mentally, it is important to have the proper tone and word choice when speaking to or about her. Always choose your words carefully. It is important that she feel safe around you. She has to be able to "let her hair down" and be her true authentic self with you. This looks different for every woman but is also true for every woman. If she cannot be herself around you, there's a level of trust missing that will bring the relationship to a standstill at some point. Women are emotional beings who need to be mentally stimulated. If you can stimulate her intellectually, you have the ability to secure her mentally.

···◆◆◆···

Time and time again, the Black woman proves how much of a force she can be in this world. Like me, if you are completely honest with yourself, you can admit that she is nothing short of amazing! She is truly a gift from God! Black women are doers in every sense of the word and that is why it is important to celebrate them. They have achieved so many monumental feats that are necessary for the success of the Black nucleus family, and the world as a whole. Where would we really be without Black women?

As you enter manhood, you will come to see how much of a contributor the Black woman is and has been to our families and the world at large. These accomplishments are extraordinary and deserve to be celebrated–this is where you come in! A real man has the ability to celebrate the accomplishments and achievement of goals produced by his Black woman without hesitation nor threat. The Black woman only poses a threat when you are against her, never for her. As a man, it is important for you to be able to applaud her whenever or wherever. You have to become her biggest cheerleader, cheering louder than anyone else in the stadium–and be comfortable in that. It does not and will never make you less of a man for cheering and celebrating your woman. When you enter holy matrimony, you will soon discover that success for one of you means success for both of you. Why not get practice at encouraging and uplifting her in the early stages of your relationship so you are positioned to continue to elevate her. Your encouragement and celebration could be the very key she needs and desires to take her to the next level.

···◆◆◆···

As I considered how a man can love a Black woman, my initial thought was, "this is easy!" Unfortunately, it is not as easy as I would have hoped. The Black woman doesn't just deserve any kind of love. She deserves a unique kind of love. One that not only introduces her to her dream come true but a love that is uniquely designed specifically for her. It speaks to all five of her love languages, in the order of importance, but exceeds her expectations. The Black woman needs to hear and see love in order for her to believe it. Once she gets the kind of love she needs, the kind of love she deserves, she will be able to fully commit. Why does she deserve such a love? Because she is worth it. This is the kind of love she puts out into the earth. The Black woman has the innate ability to put the cares, worries, and desires of everyone else around her before her very own. Time and time again, she places her own wants on the back burner to please others. She deserves nothing less than what she gives out, and more. Love her and love her well.

The Black woman deserves the world. Love her. Make her feel secure. Celebrate her. Choose your words carefully when speaking about or directly to her. Your tone and word choice are extremely important. A man contributes to the success of his woman, not the destruction. Body language is just as important as your words. The Black woman has been holding up the Black family for a very long time. She is a walking, talking outpouring of God's love for us as men. I have frequently said, "'where would we be without the Black woman," and I pray to never find out. We need her. You need her. The world needs her. As of right now, they are not aware of just how important she is. But as you continue into manhood, you will. You will see her for the amazing individual she is and treat her like a queen. Love her like Christ loved the church, and you will see an amazing change in her and yourself.

Dr. James Daniels, III

Ignite Brotherhood

Brotherhood. It's the feeling of mutual respect, love, compassion for your friends and family, and becoming deeply rooted within your community. As Black men in today's society, we must stick together and build upon our many weaknesses and strengths. We come from a bloodline of kings and leaders and have the potential to do powerful things that may seem unimaginable. It's important that you know that our culture has so much power in this country but society doesn't want you to see it. They'd rather see you do wrong or fall into false stereotypes that they placed upon you. I challenge you to show them that they are wrong and that they underestimate the power of an educated Black man… although it is what they seem to fear the most. Let's go back in time to the civil rights era and look at the Black community from a third-person perspective in comparison to now. We had brothers and sisters walking the streets across the country expressing their concerns about institutionalized racism and demanding change. It was through their combined efforts, with multiple leaders and uniting their power through boycotts and marches that the change they sought happened right before their eyes… but with a cost. Every time we've worked together, society has found ways to demonize us and pit us against each other to regain control and do things their way. The assassinations of Dr. King and Malcolm X are examples, as are putting in place laws such as the 3-strikes law to criminalize our people and send them to jail. These acts left our communities in disarray, losing the power we once had, and forgetting our history and what we fought so hard for.

Today, time is beginning to repeat itself through the Black Lives Matter movement after the constant abuse of power from men who have sworn oaths under the constitution to protect and serve. We as a community have been working together to destroy racial bias and create unity with all people and have been making great progress! The reason why I'm explaining this to you, Black man, is that I want you to know that you are powerful and through the combined efforts of building and developing a community of like-minded brothers and sisters, you are unstoppable. There is nothing in this world you cannot do or achieve. The sky is the limit because of the combined efforts of our ancestors. Society calls us slaves, thugs, and murderers but let me remind you that we are fighters for what is right and kings and queens. Throughout the full history of the Black man we fought, fought, and fought again for equality and acceptance. They told us we couldn't but somehow we did and exceeded our wildest expectations. Do you believe that we accomplished these things through individual action? No, it was a multitude of individuals who came together for a common cause that led to change. Black man, I hope to inspire your heart, mind, and soul to go out and try new things and express to another brother that you love them and are willing to do all that you can to see them succeed in life. When you carry yourself in such a manner, it inspires our brothers to go out and do the same for someone else; and the cycle will continue to repeat itself over and over again. Black man, I challenge you to inspire others, grow yourself and uplift your community. Try new things and don't be afraid to dominate and conquer. Gather a group of like-minded brothers and use your influence and platform to create change!

It's time that we take control over our destiny and break those generational curses and turn them into generational blessings for the youth and the future of our people.

Dave Hawkins

Manage Your Associations

I want to leave you with my blueprint for managing your associations.

To effectively manage your associations, you must do the following:

1. Define Association
2. Give the Purpose of the Association Its Proper Value
3. Eliminate Bad Associations
4. Cultivate and Develop Communications with Associates
5. Remind Your Associate Why Your Association Matters
6. Provide Evidence that You are Committed to the Association
7. Operate with Honesty and Integrity
8. Meet Occasionally with Associates to Reaffirm the Association
9. Manage Your Associations Like a Great Leader
10. Keep a Scoreboard to Document the Successes of the Associations

Define Association. Associations are birthed by a common purpose or interest of two people or more. Therefore, any association is connected by a goal or interest. If we manage something, that means we are in charge of it. By extension, that means we have the power and freedom to influence how good the association will be. Man, other than the creator, is the strongest force to determine how healthy and strong or how weak and poor any association will be.

Give the Purpose of the Association Its Proper Value. Identify and give value to the interests and purposes that have linked you to an association. Are the interests rooted in taking care of the community, people, or earning money? Are the interests regarding your family's health or improving education or advancing your career? Is the association due to a referral from a trusted friend or family member? Perhaps the interests are rooted in social satisfaction from belonging to a group, club, or crew or wanting to be with a very special person. The association can be due to a spiritual connection or simply expanding your network. Sometimes your interests and purposes, although it means something of value to you, can lead to bad and poor outcomes. We can have bad associations, even some that are criminal and immoral. Too often, man has committed to associations that lead him to terrible spaces and situations. Be careful!

Good or bad, there are a countless number of reasons as to why human beings have associations. Whatever connects you to another party, you have to assign value to the connecting source. If what connects you is poorly valued, you will not care to tend to the association. Let's be real. We ignore the things that we do not care much about. If you have a true interest, you will have a stronger commitment to the association.

Eliminate Bad Associations. Bad associations can terminate good associations. I have had associations with entrepreneurs, politicians, professional athletes, entertainers, and educators as well as ex-convicts, police officers, and people living destructive lifestyles. While I have never judged people for their decisions or shortcomings in life, I had to decide the degree of the association I would have with certain people. If I recognize that I do not have a common purpose with a person, then an association will not be pursued or accepted. I was cool with them, acted with respect and love in a by-a-chance meeting of the person in public, but social disengagement (staying away from them) has been my policy for the most part, simply because we lack common interests and purpose. The disengagement does not only apply to people running afoul of the law but people in a position of power who offend my principles, morals, or personal constitution.

An example of this could be a politician I know who advocates for offensive and hostile policies toward the poor or a policy that adversely affects Black men. Black men have enough challenges without someone in public office adding to the load. Because of your chosen lousy company, an association that you would love to have with someone can be terminated. The bottom line... eliminate bad associations if you want to establish good associations with others.

Cultivate and Develop Communications with Associates. Your willingness to nurture and cultivate communication lines with the other party connected to you in purpose is critical to maintaining the association. You do not want your communication with associates to be so infrequent that when they discover your name in their phone, it provokes a facial reaction of slightly squinted eyes rotated to the right and a forehead furrowed with an index finger adorning a puckered-up chin and poked out lips. This look is a look of unfamiliarity and an effort to remember who you are. If this is the person's reaction when they see your name, you are poorly managing the association. Although associations do not need daily communications, periodic communication is necessary to stay committed to the purpose and interest that created the association.

Remind Your Associate Why Your Association Matters. The other person also has to do a value assessment (an examination or investigation of something) and decide the level of investment they will put into the association. Their value assessment and management could influence your commitment to the association. So, you may have to get other parties excited and reinvigorated regarding the purpose or interest of the association. You have to remind associates why you have come together.

"We are together in purpose because we are both trying to get paid."

"We are together in purpose because I am dope! I think that you are dope, and so we need to explore where this can go as a dating couple."

"I want to be a Kappa, a Que, a Sigma, a Groove Phi, and you want to be a Black Greek, too. We can support each other in this effort."

"I want to play Division 1 ball at Duke, UNC, Syracuse, Kentucky or Boston College; you want to play Division 1 ball at Penn State, Michigan, USC, or Georgia, let's work out together, monthly."

"I want to make Black Lives Matter; you want to make Black Lives Matter, let's stay connected."

"I like to be a Black socialite and so do you; let's "stay up" on all the high-profile events so we can be in attendance."

The examples are many. Quality management of your association will rely on your ability to remind associates that your association matters.

Provide Evidence that You are Committed to the Association. Send a text message letting your associate in athletics know that you ran 5 miles, did 50 push-ups and sit-ups, and several deadlifts today. This will show that you are invested in the thing that connects you. Send your associate in panhellenic affairs a book about the Divine Nine to let them know you are studying and are committed to becoming a Black Greek Fraternity Member. Share information to your social justice and racial equity associate, highlighting the wealth gaps amongst races and ideas you've explored to lessen and close the wealth gap. Provide your associate in becoming Black social elites in the city with a calendar of prominent events "where everybody who is anybody" is going to be. Demonstrate your commitment to the association.

Operate with Honesty and Integrity. The Late Black NFL Coach, Denny Green, once said famously, "They are who we thought they were." If you deceive, manipulate, mislead or lie to your associates, you will possibly forever lose their trust and, most likely, the association. Speak honestly, be fair, just, and moral in your associations with people, which will go a long way with the other party. People love to be associated with good people. Don't play people! Don't sacrifice the goodwill people have for you by being dishonest and operating in a fashion that lacks integrity.

Meet Occasionally with Associates to Reaffirm the Association. Invest time in your calendar to go to lunch, have coffee, play ball or attend a social event with your associates. Reaffirm that you are bound in purpose, and the association that you have with the person is worthy of an in-person meeting. This in-person meeting again shows that you value the person. If you do not have time in a calendar year for an associate, you should reconsider having the association. If the association truly matters, take time to show the associate that you value the association by meeting with them.

Manage Your Associations Like A Great Leader. To lead people, successful management of associations is a must. Leaders have followers, and those followers rely on the leader's ability to sustain and conserve their association with him. When you effectively manage your associations, associates may ask or nominate you to lead. Your stewardship of their association gives them a reason to ask you to lead important initiatives.

Keep a Scoreboard to Document the Successes of the Associations. Show your associates the success you have experienced due to your association with them. Text them a picture of a check stub that their association created for you. Text a picture of yourself in your brand new fraternity jacket now that, with their association, you have accomplished your goal of joining the fraternity. Send them a picture of you and your new special friend they introduced you to. Text a picture of you shaking hands with President Barack Obama or Vice President Kamala Harris because of an event you attended in large part due to your association with your associate. Let associates know that your association with them produces good things for you and that you are thankful.

Try using these steps to successfully manage your associations.

Anthony Driggers, Ph.D

Support Others

I am writing these words to you with a sense of urgency and passion. Now is the time for all of us to start supporting one another. The times we are living in are very volatile and unpredictable, with the entire world going through chaos and turmoil. Everyone is divided and fighting one another, whether that be country against country or between the peoples within the confines of our own country. Times like this are when we need an unbreakable support system the most. And, who is better to get that support from than your fellow brothers? Historically, the Black man has never received much support from anyone else, other than the Black woman, but the Black man needs to start lending a hand to the next Black man.

Now when I say, "lend a hand," I could mean that literally or metaphorically in a variety of ways. Before we can start supporting one another, we have to earn each other's trust. So many of us have been lied to and done wrong by a fellow brother and we've taught ourselves to not trust each other. We need to start being honest with one another. I can't possibly have trust in a person that I feel is trying to get over on me or take advantage of me for their own personal gain. I can only build my trust in the honesty that you present to me. If you're honest with me, I have respect for you and if I have respect for you, that makes it easier for me to trust you. I feel confident that all of you would agree with what I just stated.

Moving forward, as that trust has grown for one another, you need to create bonds with one another in the form of fellowship, friendship, brotherhood, etc. How deep and strong those bonds go is dictated by how much you care for each other. Showing that you care for a person is very simple. Coming to visit a brother when you have free time, picking up the phone to check in on them, taking an interest in their lives and what they have going on, asking them about their overall health in all aspects whether that be physical, mental, emotional, or spiritual; these are all ways to show that you care about someone. If we care about one another deeply, we can confide things in each other that we wouldn't with a regular person or a stranger. One of the problems of the Black man is that we have a difficult time showing humility and vulnerability. I think it is accurate to say that all of us have problems and are going through something, either internally or externally. At times, the best remedy for what you are going through is to talk about it with someone that you are close to. However, Black men tend to be closed off and keep their issues bottled inside. We are too prideful to express ourselves because we are afraid of being embarrassed and we feel that voicing our problems means that we are showing weakness. I think that what makes a great man is him being able to humble himself and feel comfortable with being vulnerable and showing weakness. We have to realize that this is why we call the fellow Black men around us brothers and friends; they are here to be a listening ear for us. If I have a strong relationship with my brother, I should be able to tell him anything and he should be able to tell me anything. Neither one of us is going to put down one another and pass unnecessary judgment on each other, but we need to listen, be completely honest and upfront, and give any helpful advice if we can. As Black men, we need to learn to open up to our brothers and let them know what is going on with us because they cannot offer support to us if we keep them in the dark about what is going on.

More important than just showing support through your listening ears and words, we need to show support through our actions towards one another. There are many things you can do to support your brother and no matter how big or small the action is, it will have some sort of impact on their life. If your brother is going through tough times and can't fill up his gas tank, send some money his way if you're in a position to do so. Put in a good referral for your brother at your job if there are open positions and you believe that he is qualified for it. Also, if you find yourself on the other end of this situation, make a great impression if given the opportunity and make the most of it, so your brother can be shown in a good light for opening the door for you. If someone you're close to has just started a new business, make an effort to be one of their first supporters. Whatever service they are providing might be beneficial for you and you can continue to support them, but if it isn't for you, make use of your vast network and get your brother connected with other people in your circle that might benefit from his service. As Black men, we need to stop being selfish–only being concerned with ourselves–and become more selfless. We should want to be a blessing to others more, without being concerned about receiving something in return. I believe in the strength and workings of prayer, so remember to pray for your brother. Ask for many blessings to come upon him whether that be with his family, health, finances, house, education, job, or overall success. With everything I've just explained, the most important thing that all of us have to make sure we do is to instill this within the upcoming generations. This includes sons, grandsons, nephews, mentees, or any younger men that you are associated with. We have to be an example for them and show them the good that comes from Black men standing together with one another and supporting each other. It has to start with us, and it will be a beautiful sight to watch what we've built carry on in strength and growth for the many generations to come after us.

Ty Mapp

Seek Wise Counsel

"I did it on my own," a premise widely idealized by the hip-hop community is a lie. No one makes it on their own; there is always some level of help needed, advice taken, or breaks given. Accepting help can make the difference between failure and accomplishment but seeking it out often marks the difference between the average and the great.

Choosing not to seek out wise counsel can often be the main thing stopping one's progress. Seeking out those with great wisdom and experience not only saves time but cuts down on unnecessary failures. Tapping into the wells of knowledge attained by others allows us to slow down and process information better. Demonstrating the patience to wait for a second opinion will lead to better results.

The ability and desire to seek wise counsel are present in those that achieve at all levels. Countries come together as the United Nations to collaborate and solve worldwide issues. Every U.S. president appoints his own cabinet members, those who are highly skilled in areas where he may lack expertise. Corporations have boards of trustees and hire consultants to improve sales and customer relations. Husbands and wives help each other build a strong household and raise their children.

The most successful organizations and relationships are built on seeking wise counsel.

The conviction to actively seek and listen to wise counsel is humbling because one is essentially giving up dominion. It is letting go of the wheel for a second and letting someone else drive; it requires faith. To truly listen to and accept wise counsel you not only have to reveal that you do not have the best judgment in every situation but make this realization apparent to those you are seeking counsel from. Exposing the areas where you lack expertise and direction requires a high level of vulnerability but by doing so you can open up the possibilities provided by the wisdom of those you sought for help. It is scary and often the opposite of what we Black men have been taught our entire lives—to not show weakness, uphold the bravado, or fake it until we make it. But a Black man who can overcome his social conditioning and see the need to seek out the opportunity to receive wise counsel is one who is ambitious, driven, and dedicated to his cause. A Black man who can balance leading and being led by those wiser than himself is a man without limits.

This lesson became apparent during my junior year at Delaware State University when I started a male leadership initiative for my campus, The Faithful Black Men Association of Delaware State University. Up until this point, it was easy to lean on my wisdom (or the wisdom I thought I had). It was easy because I only needed to be concerned with leading myself but I quickly learned that as we add other people to the equation, whether it be friends or family, significant others, or team members, we can see the limited scope that our wisdom has.

When I had the idea to start the FBMA I thought it was the greatest thing in the world. I drafted the idea and concept and went straight to the President of the University with the grand yet vague promise of male achievement. Needless to say, I received a humbling "no" (the first of many in the process); however, he did grant me a meeting about a month later to hear more about the idea. In the meantime, I took this "no" to heart and realized that when trying to do something bigger than myself I needed the wisdom of a network bigger than my own experience and judgment. Humbled, I first sought out the wisdom of my peers, other male leaders on campus with resumes and lists of accomplishments as long as my own. Together we assembled teams to plan and eventually run every part of the initiative. Utilizing the wisdom of my peers, the initiative was able to grow beyond my limited understanding of the University. By seeking the wise counsel of others, we were all able to build a program that truly served the University and reached every corner of the campus.

When a few members of my team and I went to the meeting with the President a month later, the FBMA Initiative was welcomed with open arms. The President communicated that this was the type of program he intended to put in place during his presidency and subsequently put us in charge. From there, we sought the opinion and input of the administration, faculty, staff, and students, and were able to grow the program to a level of statewide recognition within a few months!

But seeking the counsel of others did not stop there. We reached out to local community leaders, pastors, corporations, and even administrators at other colleges to see how we could continue to improve the quality of this program. This much-needed lesson in collaboration and seeking the wise counsel of others remains a strong component of the initiative. And, for me, I learned to seek the wise counsel of others in nearly every area of my life; and as a result, the counsel I've received has helped me get to places and have experiences I would not have thought of had I continued to lean on my own understanding.

Don't discount the power in seeking wise counsel–in asking for help–doing so can save you from making traumatizing mistakes, shorten your learning curve, reduce your failures, increase your successes, and open doors of opportunity that you didn't know existed.

Corban Weatherspoon

Have Allies

In life, one can travel fast, or they can travel far. Moving alone has its pros. You only have to take your own thoughts into consideration, you don't have to accommodate anyone else and you don't have to wait for anyone. Sounds good, right? Unfortunately, mentally, physically, and spiritually, humans are herd animals. To learn, we go to school and study with fellow classmates. To build, someone creates a blueprint and others use those plans to construct the building. To worship, we congregate in the space of our respective higher power and give praise. For success in life, allies are necessary. With an abundance of allies, expertise, wisdom, and experience beyond your own are easily accessible.

Allies come in many forms such as mentors, co-workers, classmates, and sponsors. A mentor is an extremely valuable individual. They share from their own experience and network to drastically shorten the amount of time you must spend on research or trial and error. A good mentor will help you organize and plan for your future.

As you progress in higher education, you will have many classes and many more classmates. Classmates are powerful allies to have because they are facing the same day-to-day struggles as you. Classmates can help with studying, peer to peer mentorship, and personal favors. Between studying, working, and crafting expertise in a subject area, higher education is in no way easy. Classmates will be a lifelong network to assist you personally and professionally.

After finishing your education, you will go into the workforce. At your job, there will be employees in various roles above, below, and adjacent to your own. For co-workers in your field of expertise, collaboration is a powerful tool to excel and build knowledge of various domains. Being knowledgeable in your field will not always get you promoted and put into higher positions. People in your workplace must also know you.

A sponsor is another person you must have as an ally. Sponsors are usually people in senior or executive positions that can and will vouch for your abilities when promotions are available. High praise or acknowledgment from an executive can be a critical factor for improving your career trajectory.

Gaining allies can happen strategically or by chance, but maintaining allies always takes time and effort. Allyship is not a one-sided relationship. To gain and keep allies, you yourself must be a good ally. A good ally has several important qualities such as effective communication, great professionalism, keeps promises, and always puts forth their best efforts. Culture and language are important factors in effective communication. When speaking in the workplace, you must be tactful and concise in your speech. Convey exactly what you need to say, read the situation, and strive to add value. If conflicts do arise, prioritize resolving them at the earliest opportunity to prevent ill feelings from lingering. Make sure your word keeps its value. Try your absolute hardest to keep your end of any agreement when promises are made. If you are unable to keep your word, people will always doubt what you say. The words you say are important, but actions are what separate the good from the great.

Exemplifying professionalism is an absolute must. Professionals embody strong attributes such as loyalty, duty, respect, selfless service, honor, integrity, and personal courage. A fierce sense of duty is needed to ensure you always put forth your best efforts on individual and group projects. Outside of projects, time should be spent with allies to build comradery. This can be in the form of getting coffee, studying together, or volunteering. Finally, be sure to choose your battles wisely. You will not always agree with your allies. Attempt to negotiate with or persuade allies to your way of thinking. Regardless of the depth of the issue or the height of the reward, never back-stab an ally.

Allies come in many forms and are a catalyst for success in any venture. Each party must be intentional in their words and actions to reap the benefits of this partnership.

Job Albarr

Overcome Adversities

Before sharing what it means to overcome adversity, we should clarify what adversity means. With a quick Google® search we can find out that adversity represents "difficulties" or "misfortune," but in all honesty, adversity means so many different things for so many different people. For some people, it could be trying to make their monthly rent and for others, it could be trying to get another business off the ground. Adversity can take many forms, but despite the turmoil it causes us, adversity is actually necessary to overcome life's greatest challenges. It is how we react to adversity that determines our emotional intelligence, and it is our reaction that determines how adversity shapes us.

To illustrate how any type of adversity can have a positive or negative impact on us based upon how we react to it, I want to give you an example using my car. I love my car. It gives me the freedom to go wherever I need to at any time. I still remember when I got the car on my birthday like it was yesterday. It was one of the best days of my life and I was so excited to do things like take my friends to the movies, go to work on my own and even just go to the store whenever I wanted. There was, however, one downside. You see, when my car hasn't been driven for a long time, the back tires gradually lose air until they are pretty much flat. I have to grab the air pump and put air in my back tires before I drive anywhere; let me tell you, I don't enjoy it one bit. First, I have to find the air pump in the garage, and then I have to plug the pump into the two back tires and wait for the tires to reach their correct pressure. This process always takes up to thirty minutes and always puts a real dent in my schedule. This is an example of adversity. Not the most impactful example, but an example nonetheless. As I said, adversity comes in different forms. How I react to this instance of adversity though, will surprisingly determine how the rest of my day goes. I could easily throw in the towel, give up on trying to pump my tires, and just stay in the house. However, that action alone could mean missing out on getting paid at work. It could mean missing out on cashing a check. It could even mean missing out on a potentially fun day at the movies with my friends. Instead, no matter how tedious and grueling the task of pumping my tires is, I do it with a smile because I know how happy I am going to be with the end result. Adversity can also be a teacher of work ethic. Sometimes, you have to commit to the toil and labor necessary to get the result you want.

Now, to discuss an instance of adversity that's a bit more serious. Without going too much into any extraneous detail, my elementary school and middle school days weren't the best. I tended to do really well academically, generally getting As and Bs on most of my schoolwork. However, I did have my struggles socially. Whenever I was put in a new environment, I either kept quiet to avoid being judged or I believed that being the most outlandish person in the room would earn me friends.

Neither approach worked, and I ended up in a place socially that I resented and no longer wanted to be in. Going into high school was the point when I really wanted to work to change my image. This was going to be the moment when I finally overcame my adversity. Admittedly, it didn't work out that great at first. When I first got to high school, I still struggled to make friends. At one point, I was in such a negative place mentally that I thought this was how things were going to be forever... until I met a group of people that I could truly be myself around. As a matter of fact, I met some of my closest friends in high school. Though I still had the same issue making friends when I first got to college, I was in a good enough place mentally that it didn't bother me as much as it did in elementary and middle school. I came to the realization that no matter where I went, I would have enough sound judgment and confidence in myself that I could discern who or what was meant (or not) for me. And isn't that really what overcoming adversity is all about? Recognizing that everything is not going to be easy–even those things that are meant for you–but having the courage to face the difficulties and forge ahead to what is waiting for you on the other side. We will all experience many opportunities to lose focus, turn around, or quit in the face of adversity; however, staying positive and facing each adversity as it comes with boldness, courage and tenacity will help you to overcome even the toughest challenges in life. Maintaining a positive mindset, about any adversity and your ability to overcome it, is key to you becoming unstoppable and creating your best life.

Noah Robinson

Be A Changemaker

Brother, who said you can't make a difference? Don't ever tell yourself that. If someone ever tells you that you can't, ask them why. You have no idea yet what strength you possess inside. Those thoughts, voices, and ideas in your head are real and will be so helpful in moving forward. Remember, if you can imagine yourself doing a thing, you can make it happen.

For certain, these are strange and troubling times in this world. But it is also an opportunity to step up and be included in the conversations. But first, you must learn how the system works. All systems have basic governing principles. And in these governing rules–these policies and procedures–you will find a blueprint for creating your rules of engagement and a strategic path for making a difference.

I was told that my great-great-grandfather could read and write as a slave. The slave owners, many of whom could barely read or write themselves, used to have him write notes from their various meetings. He learned their system. When he was freed he bought 400 acres of land.

My father was a war veteran. When he came home he worked a lot of different jobs earning a living. He started his own roofing and carpentry business. But, as a Black in that era, that came with many different challenges. The challenges didn't stop him; he understood where he was and where he wanted to go. He joined the police force and was assigned to a very segregated area in the city. One night at the end of his shift he was tired of being discriminated against even as a police officer. That night he was going to quit his job because of it. As he was going to turn in his badge, another Black officer stopped him. After four hours, he got my father to change his mind about quitting. But my father made a promise to himself. The promise was that if he stayed in the police department, he would not stay as an officer. He would have to elevate himself to a higher rank. Ten years later my father became the head of that police agency as the first African American police director of a major U.S. city. In becoming the first to hold such a position, he learned the system, engaged it, and overcame the obstacles to attain it, and took a generation of minorities with him who was bound for success.

···◆◆◆···

You have dark skin and full lips. Enviously some people try to copy your beauty. Others, full of jealousy, try to say you are a bad person; trying to cause you to doubt yourself. Through this chaos, people who don't have your complexion will never be able to understand what it's like to wear Black skin. Contrary to what they think, your skin is a symbol of power and perseverance. But first, you have to believe in yourself.

Most of the time you will be fighting for a righteous cause, and in many of those fights, you will find you are fighting alone. Don't expect any kind of support to show up. Be prepared to go alone so you'll never be disappointed in others' lack of engagement. Those ideas in your head and the dreams you have of being better and helping others are the first steps to achieving your goals. Once again, if you're going to fight, know the process in order to win. The weapon undoubtedly is your mind. Learn any system and how it works.

I'm a lifelong resident of the bricks of the city streets. And in those bricks, there are many obstacles that you'll have to overcome to make it and to make a difference. Remember you have power and you come from powerful people.

···•♦•···

I remember promising my mother not to go on the North side of town in fear of the unchecked vigilante groups that roamed that side of the city letting the people of color know they shouldn't move there.

I remember riding my bike in the neighboring towns and being called the "N" word.

I remember being in my teens walking from a neighboring town's shopping area and being stopped by the police in broad daylight and asked where I'm coming from.

I remember being the guy in a crowd of people exiting the mall who is the only one stopped at the door by the security guard to have my bag checked. I said that I have receipts. His response was "yeah, I know; if not you would have run out the door already." Really dude?

In spite of these experiences and more, I wanted to make a difference, so I entered the police academy. In the academy, there was a very racist police recruit in my class who joked with some of the other classmates that he doesn't have a problem with Blacks because he keeps three in his basement.

Even after becoming a police officer, I would still have a bit of anxiety when stopped for "driving while Black." Because I was an officer, I could ask why they were stopping me and avoid the bogus allegations and traffic summonses.

While striving to make a difference, I saw the overreach of young white police officers, most of whom never associated with people of color, making jokes and finding joy when arresting people of color.

I watched the administration demand more tickets on claims of inefficiency, causing police officers of all colors to abuse the communities of minorities with a flood of arrests and traffic summonses. The arrests turn into fines and generate revenue for the city but the arrest records prevent minorities from getting better jobs.

When I embraced the religion of Islam, I was continually attacked by the police agency for believing differently, to the point that we as Muslim officers filed a religious discrimination lawsuit that rose to the United States Supreme Court. Again, if you're going to fight, know how the system works so you can work within the system to make a difference.

I penned an article following the Juvenile Justice Commission's lead on the "stationhouse adjustment" declaring that the more exposure juveniles had to the justice system the easier it would be for them to acclimate to incarceration. That year, of the 1200 juveniles arrested within the city, over 1000 of them were young Black children. This is how they block our path long before we get started.

I sued my beloved police agency and city over a powerful tyrannical police subculture that existed for 15 years. The subculture, immune from civil or criminal liability, used the weight of the municipal government against any employee who would speak out against it through a system of retaliation and termination. An extensive dossier on the internal disparate treatment was provided along with examples of external disparate treatment which helped to formalize the current federal monitoring of the police agency.

I sued a major corporation for religious oppression and persecution. The lawsuit brought by the Equal Employment Opportunity Commission caused an agency-wide change of policy which prevented the corporation from oppressing its workers financially to support their beliefs.

I have given countless seminars in my community on what to do when stopped by the police. It is an unfortunate necessity in my community.

I participated as a guest lecturer at local community colleges about community policing and its subcultures.

I created local study group classes for minorities to prepare to take the police exam to try and change what policing represents in the community.

My early experiences could have jaded me and caused me to be more concerned about preserving my little corner of the world. But brother, I recognized that we must shoulder the burden for those coming after us. You can't allow yourself to be distracted by trivial things in your environment or people or situations designed to take you off course and delay your progress. You have to stay on course to grow up and become a man and a father. The father that sets the tone and creates boundaries for his children, preparing them to make a difference in the world in their own way. The man that values community and uses his knowledge, experience, network, and other resources to bring about positive change. Being a changemaker does not have to entail a grandiose gesture or be a long and challenging task. You can make a difference and impact change in small ways every day. You have brothers on the same road ahead of you. Ask them and they will show you the way.

Yes, brother, for certain you can change things. And, if not you, who?

Anthony Kerr

Foster Unity

A new African American proverb has taken root; although its content and meaning we should already understand and know. Simply stated by Haiti Madhubuti, "A nation that uses *I* instead of *we* is dispersed and in trouble." This is true on every level of life. Society is built on the collectiveness of its members. Family, community, states, nations and empires all rise or fall depending on whether the principles of unity are inherent or inherited.

The unity of a chain is what gives it strength. A weak or broken link weakens the whole. There is strength in unity.

The history of most cultures of mankind includes a struggle for a unified existence whether obtained by war, peaceful diplomacy or because of a dependency on existing clans, tribes, or nations. So, too, in this age, the Black man must engage in the strongest possible form of a unified people.

Umoja–meaning Unity–a Swahili term, must be one of the basic ideologies of African people throughout the African diaspora. We must ask ourselves what unity truly means. I believe unity means and provides a path to freedom. What then is freedom? It is the power or right to act or think without hindrance or restraint. It is argued that we, as Black people, have obtained such freedom. If this were so, then why is the number one weapon that has been used time and time again still in play? In fact, I could argue that it has been in play since the beginning of mankind–DIVIDE AND CONQUER! Create disunity and distrust within a community and an enemy's goals are halfway won. Division is a powerful tool against those with vision.

Unity is one key in unlocking chains binding a people who are struggling to obtain freedom mentally, materially, spiritually, or physically.

It was once asked, "What ethnic group is the worst enemy of the Black man, and what ethnic group is his best friend?" Expecting an answer identifying this or that ethnic group (Jews, Arabs, Englishmen, Irish, etc), I heard, "We have been our own best friend and our own worst enemy!"

Again, division and disunity may "do us in." One must understand what el-Hajj Malik el-Shabazz's, more commonly known as Malcom X, analogy of the house negro and field negro has to say to us as a people. He explained that the house negro's life with his slave master made him more akin to the slave master than his brothers in the field. The house negro no longer saw his plight tied to that of the field negro but to the fate of his slave master. Our disunity kept us oppressed and controlled by the enemy. Malcom X warned us that this mentality has perpetuated to modern times and keeps us separated from one another today.

Thus, in these most stressful and difficult times, it is imperative that we get a renewed understanding of Umoja; that a house divided against itself cannot stand. This is a spiritual perspective that would be ideal for use by all societies of man.

The family is the basis of our unity. When we can see each other as members of an extended family, we become much closer to being free. Next comes community. And while at times we don't all agree on the issues, or how to address them, it is a commitment to mutual respect and love between our brothers and sisters that will allow us to unite against a common threat. Unity, friendship, and brotherhood are what will empower us to overcome all weapons formed against us.

> "And let your best be for your friend. If he must know the ebb of your tide, let him know its flood also. For what is your friend that you should seek him with hours to kill? Seek him always with hours to live."

Khalil Gibran

Tyrone Roosevelt

Give of Yourself

Growing up in the South was a humbling experience, especially during the holidays. Having been raised by my grandmother, I cherished the love she gave me as I knew her love for me was unconditional. According to the U.S. Census Bureau, my family, whom I thought had all we needed and more, was actually living in poverty although it did not feel that way to me. We lived in a rural area in South Carolina thirty minutes from the nearest town. The woods were thick and never-ending, populated with cedar, oak, pine, and other trees and shrubs. During the Christmas holidays, we would rush into the woods to select the perfect tree in our eyes—a five-foot pine tree that had little resemblance to a traditional Christmas tree—careful to avoid poisonous snakes that we became surprisingly used to seeing from time to time without fear. It's fascinating how you can get accustomed to something that could snuff your life out in an instant and not fear it but other things like a math test or speaking in front of a classroom of your peers instills petrifying fear. We would meticulously prune the tree with a bush axe and prepare it for our journey back to the house simply by dragging it to the space it would occupy in our modest living room. Once the tree was upright and placed in position, we would stabilize it in what was called a foot tub filled with dirt. Next, we would put large inexpensive lights on the tree and of course, we could not forget the tinsel. Anxious, each Christmas, I would wake up early in the morning to see what my grandmother said Santa had brought me as I had an ambivalence about whether Santa was real or not. Nevertheless, it did not matter as I was about to get my yearly treats. Each year I would look forward to what I would get for Christmas, a bicycle, a fire engine, toy soldiers, cowboy outfits, or another fun toy. "Me, me, me," I thought. This made me very happy.

Now, after having grown up with those experiences ingrained in me and being used to getting gifts at Christmas time, I met my wonderful wife who grew up with thirteen brothers and sisters. Her Christmas experiences were much different than mine. She never received a toy or had a Christmas like the ones I joyfully experienced. This opened my eyes and I realized that I needed to reevaluate my value system. It is not all about me, me, me or mine, mine, mine and get, get, get! It is about giving to those in need and those that are less fortunate.

On December 23, 2011, in Walterboro S.C., my wife and I hosted a Christmas party for one hundred less fortunate families who could not afford a gift for their kids at Christmas. The event was the first of its kind in the town and was advertised on the front page of the local newspaper, which I thought was a good thing as we wanted more families in need to know that we wanted them to be involved in the festivities. The opportunity to give to those one-hundred-plus families gave me a feeling of gratitude that I had never experienced before in my life. I believe the greatest gift is to give of yourself.

Dr. Martin Luther King, Jr. was a spiritual man, a prolific writer, and he gave much of himself, so much so that it led to his untimely demise. Let us explore four thoughts on giving back from Dr. King:

1. *"Every man must decide whether he will walk in the light of creative altruism or in the darkness of destructive selfishness."*

   Essentially, Dr. King was saying you are one or the other; generous or selfish. It has been said that 2020 was the worst year in our lifetime with food lines, high unemployment, COVID-19, and more. We must all ask ourselves what we can do during these hard times to help others. Once we get the answer, then we should act. My wife and I have partnered with a team that feeds the homeless in Washington D.C. We visited home-less shelters to provide clothes to the less fortunate. One thing we have realized is that you can't out-give God. It seems like the more we give, the more we get in return; it is truly amazing. Find ways to give that are meaning-ful for the receiver. The Universe will somehow return your generosity.

2. *"We are prone to judge success by the index of our salaries or the size of our automobiles rather than by the quality of our service and relationship to mankind."*

   Although it is important to make a good salary to live a comfortable life, it is not the universal measure of your success. A person who decides to become a teacher is a success. A person who decides to become a stay-at-home parent to raise their child is a success. Success is a thing that you decide to do and you do it well. Often this is providing a service to others. The size of your automobile and other material things may often signify debt more than success. Don't be measured by material gains. Be measured by the value you add to other people's lives as this is priceless.

3. *"Everyone has the power for greatness not for fame but greatness, because greatness is determined by service."*

   Robert Frederick Smith is arguably the wealthiest Black philanthropist at a net worth of $5 billion according to Forbes. He is a businessman, chemical engineer, and investor. He gives millions of dollars to education. Mr. Smith paid off the student debt for the entire graduating class at Morehouse College. He would qualify as having achieved greatness, I think. No, not everyone who is great is exceedingly wealthy. The important thing to remember is the service you provide to others is where greatness is born.

4. *"The first question which the priest and the Levite asked was, if I stop to help this man, what will happen to me? But the Good Samaritan reversed the question, if I do not stop to help this man, what will happen to him?"*

   During the late 90s, I lived in the Harlem pre-gentrification era. I was going home one evening after work and I saw three young men in their late teens on a nearby block. Two of the young men pounced on the one and commenced beating him down with a vengeance. I did not know these young men. In fact, I had never seen them on that block before that day. As bystanders scurried by in a haste to reach safety with little or no concern for the victim, I looked in awe. This is the way I witnessed it as no one lifted a finger to assist the young man. I immediately parked my car, got out, and made my way to the scene. I asked what was going on and if everything was okay. I was told "Mister, this doesn't concern you so go 'bout your business!" I said, "I'm making it my business." Once again, the young men said, "I done told you to go on 'bout your business." By this time the *flight or fight* response was having an internal battle within me. I was determined to do something so, although reluctant, I felt compelled to listen to my less reasonable self... fight, if necessary. I approached the victim and pulled him from their grasp vigorously and with authority and yelled, "Stop it now! This is not going down on my watch!" I was shocked as they stopped and allowed me to take him away without any further altercation. I quickly took the bloody gentleman inside the building and asked the desk clerk inside to assist him. The young man was incredibly grateful and could not stop thanking me. I told him he was welcome and went on my way. What I did was risky and dangerous so I don't recommend putting yourself in harm's way but find a way to help someone in need. If I did not stop to help that young man what would have happened to him?

As alluded to earlier, giving of myself is one of the most rewarding experiences I have ever had the pleasure of having.

Few people can give like Robert Smith, Oprah Winfrey, Denzel Washington, and the likes but you don't have to. Give of your time. Be there to listen to someone in need. Be kind to people and treat them the way you would like to be treated. Listen to your heart and your head and when it comes time to give, somehow you will know the best way to do so. Be mindful that at times it may be subtle and other times it may be obvious, but that internal nudging will be there nonetheless; so listen, listen, listen and give, give, give!

Alfred Robinson

Notes

1. https://www.dictionary.com/browse/visionary

2. https://www.dictionary.com/browse/of?s=t

3. *Spaceballs.* Mel Brooks.Metro-Goldwyn-Mayer, 1987. Motion Picture.

4. https://www.merriam-webster.com/dictionary/strength

5. http://blackstarproject.org/index.php/advocacy-organizing/circulate-black-dollars-in-black-community.html

6. Ballard, Glenn, and Siedah Garrett. Booklet. "The Man in the Mirror." *Bad,* BMG Rights Management, Universal Music Publishing Group, 1988.

7. https://www.studylight.org/lexicons/eng/hebrew/120.html

8. https://www.differencebetween.com/difference-between-ethical-and-vs-moral/

9. https://www.wrvo.org/post/illegal-farm-worker-becomes-brain-surgeon#stream/0

10. The Biblical Counseling Reference Guide, by June Hunt, p. 214

11. *Black's Law Dictionary, 2nd edition, published in 1910*

12. https://www.gotquestions.org/Bible-overcomer.html

13. https://www.cancer.org/content/dam/cancer-org/research/cancer-facts-and-statistics/cancer-facts-and-figures-for-african-americans/cancer-facts-and-figures-for-african-americans-2019-2021.pdf

14. "Keep Ya Head Up" by Tupac Shakur (2Pac). Album: Strictly for My N.I.G.G.A.Z., released February 16, 1993 under Interscope Records.

Our Authors

Aaron Jeter   Father, Educator, Runner, Reader

Aaron-Eugene A. Pair   Healthcare Professional; Founder & CEO, Pair Technology LLC

Abdullah Jose   Poet, Author, Alchemist

Alfred Robinson   Founder & CEO, Masters Global Empowerment Group Inc.

Andre' Valines   Founder & CEO Brother 4 Brother Mentoring Services

Anthony Driggers, Ph.D   Executive Director, Options Without Walls

Anthony Kerr   Same road, just in front of you.

Anthony Mapp   Pastor

Anwar Miller   Speaker, Self-Development Coach, Entrepreneur

Barry D. Ford   Founder & CEO, GETFIT4LIFE Training Association

Calvin O. Griffin   Father, Brother, Mentor, Coach, Founder

Channon L. Rothmiller   Writer and Friend

Chris Brooks	Grateful Worker and Tireless Father
Corban Weatherspoon	Student of Life, Son of God
D. Michael Edge, Ed.D	Father, Educator; CEO, D-Edge Tax Service LLC
Dave Hawkins	Brother
DT Stanley	Pastor, Harvest Time Worship Center
Eric D. Brown	Dude Among Dudes
Gary Walker	Father, Brother, Friend
H. Eugene L. Pair	Husband, Father, Educator, Entrepreneur
Isaac Brown Jr	Author, Creative Writer
James C. Daniels III, Ed.D	Educator, Founder & CEO, Don't Judge Me Productions
James Pair	Founder & CEO Zuberi Health
Job Albarr	Software Engineer
Jordan Spencer	Friend
K. Darren Diggs	Musician, Percussionist, Outlaw
Kevin Walker	Licensed Professional Counselor
Lamont Hale	Program Director & COO, CAAGKC
Marco M. L. Robinson	Author
Melvin Sarpey	CEO, Sarpey Realty LLC
Nick Joseph	Haitian-American Leader

Noah Robinson	Son, Brother, Friend
Orin Solomon	President of Marketing
Roger Okewole	Christian, Father, Husband, Brother, Son, Engineer, Artist
Steven A. Johnson, MD, FACS	Director, Surgery and Surgical Critical Care
Ty Mapp	Brother
Tyrone Roosevelt	Poet
Wali W. Rushdan II, Esquire	Community leader, Lawyer, Mentor, Father, Husband

The Compilers

Anwar Miller

Anwar Miller has more than 20 years of experience as an entrepreneur, trainer, speaker, and self-development coach. He has also honed his leadership skills and business acumen as a corporate professional in the software industry. Consulting with C-Level and senior executives of Fortune 500 companies, he helps companies to define and execute on customer experience strategies to meet their corporate objectives. His portfolio of clients has included companies such as Nikon, Sirius XM, Subaru, BMW, Mercedes-Benz, and Avis Budget Group. He is now a Strategic Account Executive with Google helping C-level executives to execute their technology strategy.

Anwar was first inspired towards entrepreneurship as an undergraduate student at North Carolina Agricultural & Technical State University. It was during his sophomore year that Anwar had the opportunity to meet successful business owners and entrepreneurs that he aspired to emulate. In tandem with the completion of his Bachelor of Science in Electrical Engineering,

Anwar spent the majority of his college years developing his own marketing and sales company, RAW Team Marketing.

RAW Team Marketing is an independent contractor of ACN, which is the world's largest direct seller of telecommunications, energy and essential services for home and business. Today, RAW Team Marketing has grown to over $26,000,000 in annual billing revenue with 80,000 customers across seven countries.

Through the trials and triumphs of developing his own lucrative enterprise, combined with the savvy of an extensive career in the software industry, Anwar has learned the cornerstones of building a successful business, and he passionately commits his efforts to training, teaching and inspiring others to achieve their dreams. From audiences as small as one to as large as 25,000 people, Anwar's unique style and witty delivery leaves a lasting impression that embeds the core principles of his message in the minds of his audience. Anwar continuously strives to attain new heights in his vocational endeavors while he pursues his lifetime commitment to his own personal development in earnest.

Anwar draws his strength from his foundation of faith and his motivation to excel from his family. His greatest fulfillment comes from his thriving marriage of 20 years to Lois and the legacy that he is building through his three beautiful children, Safiya, Jalyn, and Solomon.

Corban Weatherspoon

Corban Weatherspoon is a senior at Delaware State University majoring in Bioengineering. He has been heavily involved in leadership activities focused on the development of men. He held the presidency of M.O.C.A. (Men of Color Alliance) for two years and envisioned and led the collaborative initiative Faithful Black Men's Association of Delaware State University; working closely with administration and corporations to help bring opportunities to the young men on campus. Beyond these leadership roles, Corban is an Honors College student and has served as a Peer Counselor, Teal Fellow, and Honors Ambassador.

Academically, he earned and maintained status as a Presidential Scholar throughout his enrollment, consistently earning Dean's List and other academic recognitions. He has been selected as an HBCU Competitiveness Scholar by the White House Initiative on HBCUs through the U.S. Department of Education, twice named a Thurgood Marshall College Fund Scholar, completed the Harvard Business School Virtual Venture into Management program and the Summer Institute for Emerging Managers and Leaders through the University of California San Diego.

Corban's work experience includes internships at the OSCAR Research Lab and the Biomechanics Lab, both at Delaware State University, Alfred I. DuPont Hospital for Children/Nemours Research, UTP University of Sciences and Technology in Bydgoszcz, Poland, the Jupiter Laser Facility at Lawrence Livermore National Laboratory in Livermore, California, and the NYC Architectural Biennial (Virtual). He also completed the First

Founders Accelerator where he built and presented a fintech start-up solution to address current societal financial issues facing his peers.

Corban credits his parents, Gary and Dr. Cherita Weatherspoon along with his University for much of his success and hopes to progress to a position in life that allows him to give back to his community in multiple ways.

Brought to You by

THE IUME WORDS PROJECT
INSPIRE . UPLIFT . MOTIVATE . EMPOWER

An initiative of Spoonfed Motivation Media®
Learn more at
www.SpoonfedMotivation.com

Made in the USA
Middletown, DE
26 May 2021